Sadlier

WE⊕BELIEVE™

Jesus
Shares
God's
Life

Grade Two

Sadlier
A Division of William H. Sadlier, Inc.

Nihil Obstat

Reverend John G. Stillmank, S.T.L.
Censor Librorum

Imprimatur

✠ Most Reverend William H. Bullock
Bishop of Madison
November 25, 2002

The *Nihil Obstat* and *Imprimatur* are official declarations that a book or pamphlet is free of doctrinal or moral error. No implication is contained therein that those who have granted the *Nihil Obstat* and *Imprimatur* agree with the contents, opinions, or statements expressed.

Acknowledgments

Excerpts from the English translation of the *Catechism of the Catholic Church* for the United States of America, copyright © 1994, United States Catholic Conference, Inc.—Libreria Editrice Vaticana. English translation of the *Catechism of the Catholic Church: Modifications from the Editio Typica* copyright © 1997, United States Catholic Conference, Inc.—Libreria Editrice Vaticana. Used with permission.

Scripture excerpts are taken from the *New American Bible* with *Revised New Testament and Psalms* Copyright © 1991, 1986, 1970, Confraternity of Christian Doctrine, Inc., Washington, D.C. Used with permission. All rights reserved. No part of the *New American Bible* may be reproduced by any means without permission in writing from the copyright owner.

Excerpts from the English translation of *Rite of Baptism for Children* © 1969, International Committee on English in the Liturgy, Inc. (ICEL); excerpts from the English translation of *Lectionary for Mass* © 1969, 1981, ICEL; excerpts from the English translation of *The Roman Missal* © 1973, ICEL; excerpts from the English translation of *Rite of Penance* © 1974, ICEL; excerpts from the English translation of *Rite of Confirmation*, Second Edition © 1975, ICEL; excerpts from the English translation of *A Book of Prayers* © 1982, ICEL; excerpts from the English translation of *Book of Blessings* © 1988, International Committee on English in the Liturgy, Inc. All rights reserved.

Excerpts from *Catholic Household Blessings and Prayers* Copyright © 1988, United States Catholic Conference, Inc., Washington, D.C. Used with permission. All rights reserved.

English translation of the Glory to the Father, Lord's Prayer, Apostles' Creed by the International Consultation on English Texts. (ICET)

Excerpt from Mark Twain, *Card sent to the Young People's Society, Greenpoint Presbyterian Church, Brooklyn [February 16, 1901]*.

Excerpt from survey, *Most Recent Church Membership Trend*, March 18–20, 2002, The Gallup Organization, Princeton, NJ. Permission granted.

The poem "Language of God," from *Journey Through Heartsongs*, Mattie J. T. Stepanek. Copyright © 2001, Mattie J. T. Stepanek. Reprinted with permission from VSP Books/Hyperion Books for Children.

"We Believe, We Believe in God," © 1979, North American Liturgy Resources (NALR), 5536 NE Hassalo, Portland, OR 97213. All rights reserved. Used with permission. "Sing for Joy," © 1999, Bernadette Farrell. Published by OCP Publications, 5536 NE Hassalo, Portland, OR 97213. All rights reserved. Used with permission. "Yes, We Will Do What Jesus Says," © 1993, Daughters of Charity and Christopher Walker. Published by OCP Publications, 5536 NE Hassalo, Portland, OR 97213. All rights reserved. Used with permission. "We Celebrate with Joy," © 2000, Carey Landry. Published by OCP Publications, 5536 NE Hassalo, Portland, OR 97213. All rights reserved. Used with permission. "We Come to Ask Forgiveness," © 1986, Carey Landry and North American Liturgy Resources. All rights reserved. "Stay Awake," © 1988, 1989, 1990, Christopher Walker. Published by OCP Publications, 5536 NE Hassalo, Portland, OR 97213. All rights reserved. Used with permission. "We Remember You," © 1999, Bernadette Farrell. Published by OCP Publications, 5536 NE Hassalo, Portland, OR 97213. All rights reserved. Used with permission. "God Is Here," © 1990, Carey Landry and North American Liturgy Resources (NALR), 5536 NE Hassalo, Portland, OR 97213. All rights reserved. Used with permission. "Alleluia, We Will Listen," © 1997, Paul Inwood. Published by OCP Publications, 5536 NE Hassalo, Portland, OR 97213. All rights reserved. Used with permission. "We Believe," © 1988, Christopher Walker. Published by OCP Publications, 5536 NE Hassalo, Portland, OR 97213. All rights reserved. Used with permission. Verse text © ICEL. "A Gift from Your Children," © 1992, Nancy Bourassa and Carey Landry. All rights reserved. "Jesus, You Are Bread for Us," © 1988, Christopher Walker. Published by OCP Publications, 5536 NE Hassalo, Portland, OR 97213. All rights reserved. Used with permission. "Take the Word of God with You," text © 1991, James Harrison. Music © 1991, Christopher Walker. Text and music published by OCP Publications, 5536 NE Hassalo, Portland, OR 97213. All rights reserved. Used with permission. "We Are Yours, O Lord," © 1996, Janet Vogt. Published by OCP Publications, 5536 NE Hassalo, Portland, OR 97213. All rights reserved. Used with permission. "Alleluia, We Will Listen," © 1997, Paul Inwood. Published by OCP Publications, 5536 NE Hassalo, Portland, OR 97213. All rights reserved. Used with permission. "God Has Made Us a Family," © 1986, Carey Landry and North American Liturgy Resources (NALR), 5536 NE Hassalo, Portland, OR 97213. All rights reserved. Used with permission. "Rejoice in the Lord Always," this arrangement © 1975, North American Liturgy Resources. All rights reserved. "Sing Hosanna," © 1997, Jack Miffleton. Published by OCP Publications, 5536 NE Hassalo, Portland, OR 97213. All rights reserved. Used with permission. "Litany of Saints," © 1992, John Schiavone. Published by OCP Publications, 5536 NE Hassalo, Portland, OR 97213. All rights reserved. Used with permission. "A Circle of Love," © 1991, Felicia Sandler. Published by OCP Publications. All rights reserved. "God Made the World," © 1997, Jack Miffleton. Published by OCP Publications, 5536 NE Hassalo, Portland, OR 97213. All rights reserved. Used with permission. "This Is the Day," Text: Irregular; Based on Psalm 118:24; adapt. by Les Garrett. Text and music © 1967, Scripture in Song (a division of Integrity Music, Inc.). All rights reserved.

William H. Sadlier, Inc.
9 Pine Street
New York, NY 10005-1002

ISBN: 0-8215-5402-6
6789/09 08 07 06

The Ad Hoc Committee to Oversee the Use of the Catechism,
United States Conference of Catholic Bishops,
has found this catechetical text, copyright 2004,
to be in conformity with the *Catechism of the Catholic Church*.

The Sadlier *We Believe* Program was developed by nationally recognized experts in catechesis, curriculum, and child development. These teachers of the faith and practitioners helped us to frame every lesson to be age-appropriate and appealing. In addition, a team including respected catechetical, liturgical, pastoral, and theological experts shared their insights and inspired the development of the program.

The Program is truly based on the wisdom of the community, including:

Gerard F. Baumbach, Ed.D.
Executive Vice President and Publisher

Carole M. Eipers, D.Min.
Director of Catechetics

Catechetical and Liturgical Consultants

Reverend Monsignor John F. Barry
Pastor, American Martyrs Parish
Manhattan Beach, CA

Sister Linda Gaupin, CDP, Ph.D.
Director of Religious Education
Diocese of Orlando

Mary Jo Tully
Chancellor, Archdiocese of Portland

Reverend Monsignor John M. Unger
Assoc. Superintendent for Religious Education
Archdiocese of St. Louis

Curriculum and Child Development Consultants

Brother Robert R. Bimonte, FSC
Former Superintendent of Catholic Education
Diocese of Buffalo

Gini Shimabukuro, Ed.D.
Associate Director/Associate Professor
Institute for Catholic Educational Leadership
School of Education, University of
San Francisco

Catholic Social Teaching Consultants

John Carr
Secretary, Department of Social Development
and World Peace, USCCB

Joan Rosenhauer
Coordinator, Special Projects
Department of Social Development and
World Peace, USCCB

Inculturation Consultants

Reverend Allan Figueroa Deck, SJ, Ph.D.
Executive Director, Loyola Institute for
Spirituality, Orange, CA

Kirk Gaddy
Principal, St. Katharine School
Baltimore, MD

Reverend Nguyễn Việt Hưng
Vietnamese Catechetical Committee

Dulce M. Jiménez-Abreu
Director of Spanish Programs
William H. Sadlier, Inc.

Scriptural Consultant

Reverend Donald Senior, CP, Ph.D., S.T.D.
Member, Pontifical Biblical Commission
President, The Catholic Theological Union
Chicago, IL

Theological Consultants

Most Reverend Edward K. Braxton, Ph.D., S.T.D.
Official Theological Consultant
Bishop of Lake Charles

Norman F. Josaitis, S.T.D.
Staff Theologian, William H. Sadlier, Inc.

Reverend Joseph A. Komonchak, Ph.D.
Professor, School of Religious Studies
The Catholic University of America

Most Reverend Richard J. Malone, Th.D.
Auxiliary Bishop, Archdiocese of Boston

Sister Maureen Sullivan, OP, Ph.D.
Assistant Professor of Theology
St. Anselm College, Manchester, NH

Mariology Consultant

Sister M. Jean Frisk, ISSM, S.T.L.
International Marian Research Institute
Dayton, OH

Media/Technology Consultants

Sister Caroline Cerveny, SSJ, D.Min.
Director of Educational Learning Technology
William H. Sadlier, Inc.

Sister Judith Dieterle, SSL
Past President, National Association of
Catechetical Media Professionals

Sister Jane Keegan, RDC
Editor in Chief, CyberFaith.com
William H. Sadlier, Inc.

Writing/Development Team

Moya Gullage

Rosemary K. Calicchio
Editorial Director

Lee Hlavacek
Product Developer

Mary Ann Trevaskiss
Grade Level Manager

Blake Bergen

Joanna Dailey

James P. Emswiler

Maureen Gallo

Kathy Hendricks

Gloria Hutchinson

Mary Ellen Kelly

Marianne Lenihan

James T. Morgan, Ed.D.

Daniel Sherman

Joanne Winne

Sadlier Consulting Team

Patricia Andrews
Director of Religious Education,
Our Lady of Lourdes Church,
Slidell, LA

Eleanor Ann Brownell, D.Min.
Vice President, Religion

Michaela M. Burke
Director of Consultant Services

Judith A. Devine
National Sales Consultant

Sister Helen Hemmer, IHM
Religion Consultant for
Spiritual Formation

William M. Ippolito
Executive Projects Director

Saundra Kennedy, Ed.D.
Consultant Training Specialist

Marie Murphy, Ph.D.
National Religion Consultant

Karen Ryan
Executive Researcher

John M. Stack
National Consultant

Publishing Operations Team

Deborah Jones
Director of Publishing Operations

Vince Gallo
Creative Director

Francesca Moore
Associate Art Director

Jim Saylor
Photo Editor

Design/Photo Staff
Andrea Brown, Kevin Butler, Ana
Jouvin, Sasha Khorovsky, Susan
Ligertwood, Maria Pia Marrella,
Zaniah Renner, David Rosenberg,
Bob Schatz, Debrah Wilson

Production Staff
Diane Ali, Monica Bernier,
Barbara Brown, Suzan Daley,
Tresse DeLorenzo, Arthur Erberber,
Joyce Gaskin, Eileen Gewirtzman,
Peter Herrmann, Maria Jimenez,
Sommer Keller, Miriam Lippman,
Vinny McDonough, John Mealy,
Yolanda Miley, Maureen Morgan,
Julie Murphree, Walter Norfleet,
Monica Reece, Martin Smith,
Sintora Vanderhorst

Contents

UNIT 2 Jesus Calls Us to Penance and Reconciliation

WE·BELIEVE

The *We Believe* program will help us to

learn

celebrate

share

and

live our Catholic faith.

Throughout the year we will hear about many saints and holy people.

Saint Brigid

Saint Catherine of Siena

Saint Elizabeth Ann Seton

Saint Frances Cabrini

Saint Frances of Rome

Saint Francis of Assisi

Saint John Bosco

Saint Joseph

Saint Martin de Porres

Mary, Mother of God

Saint Peter

Saint Paul

Saint Philip Neri

Saint Rose of Lima

Together, let us grow as a community of faith.

Welcome!

✝ We Gather in Prayer

Leader: Welcome everyone to Grade 2 *We Believe*.
As we begin each chapter, we gather in prayer.
We pray to God together.

Let us sing the *We Believe* song!

🎵 We Believe, We Believe in God

We believe in God;
We believe, we believe in Jesus;
We believe in the Spirit
who gives us life.

We believe, we believe
in God.

When we see **We Gather** we come together as a class.

When we see **We Believe** we learn more about our Catholic faith.

Each day we learn more about God.

WE GATHER

We begin by taking a moment to pray.

✝ *Thank you, God, for all our classmates.*

Then we

think about
talk about
write about
draw about
act out

Life

at home
in our neighborhood
at school
in our parish
in our world

Talk about your life right now.

What groups do you belong to?

Why do you like to be a member of these groups?

WE BELIEVE

We learn about

- God the Father, God the Son, and God the Holy Spirit
- Jesus, the Son of God who became one of us
- the Church and its teachings.

We find out about the different ways Catholics live their faith and celebrate God's love.

 is an open Bible. When we see it, or something like this (John 13:34), we hear the word of God.

Each of these signs points out something special that we are going to do.

means that we will make the sign of the cross and pray as we begin our lesson.

Key Word means it is time to review the important words we have learned in the day's lesson.

means we have an activity. We might

talk   write   act
   draw
       sing
work together   imagine

There are all kinds of activities! We might see in any part of our day's lesson. Be on the lookout!

♫ means it's time to sing! We sing songs we know, make up our own songs, and sing along with those in our *We Believe* music program.

As Catholics...

Here we discover something special about our faith. Don't forget to read it!

WE RESPOND

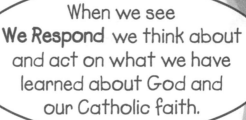

When we see **We Respond** we think about and act on what we have learned about God and our Catholic faith.

We can respond by

- thinking about ways our faith affects the things we say and do

- sharing our thoughts and feelings

- praying to God.

Then in our homes, neighborhood, school, parish, and world, we can say and do the things that show love for God and others.

In this space, draw yourself as a *We Believe* second grader.

We are so happy you are with us!

Review

Here we answer questions about what we have learned in this chapter.

Reflect & Pray

We take a few moments to think about our faith and to pray.

Key Words

We review each of the Key Words.

Review

Grade 2
Chapter 1

Circle the correct answer.

1. The Holy Family is Jesus, Mary and _____ .

   the Holy Spirit   Joseph

2. The name _____ means "God saves."

   Jesus   Trinity

3. Jesus brought the _____ that God loves all people.

   good news   sad news

4. Jesus taught us that God is with us _____ .

   sometimes   always

Use your own words to complete the sentence.

5. The three Persons in the Blessed Trinity are

   _____

   _____

   _____

ASSESSMENT Write sentences or draw pictures to tell some ways that Jesus showed God's love.

28

We Respond in Faith

Reflect & Pray

Jesus wants us to talk to him when we are feeling worried or upset. He also wants us to share with him when we are happy. Write something that you want to tell Jesus.

_____

_____

Key Words

Holy Family (p. 20)
divine (p. 25)
Blessed Trinity (p. 26)

Remember

- God the Father sent his Son, Jesus, to be with us.
- Jesus is human like us.
- Jesus did things only God can do.
- Jesus, the Son of God, taught us about God the Father and God the Holy Spirit.

OUR CATHOLIC LIFE

We Respect All People

God the Father created all people. God wants us to respect every person on earth. Many times it is easy to remember to show respect for those who are older than we are. Sometimes we find it hard to remember to show respect for people who are our age or younger, who speak another language, or who seem different from us.

You can show respect this week by being kind to your classmates. You can help a younger brother, sister, cousin, or neighbor.

Remember

We recall the four main faith statements of the chapter.

ASSESSMENT

We do a chapter activity that will show that we have discovered more about our Catholic faith.

OUR CATHOLIC LIFE

Here we read an interesting story about the ways people make the world better by living out their Catholic faith.

15

SHARING FAITH
with My Family

At the end of each chapter, you'll bring a page like this home to share with your family.

Sharing What I Learned

Talk about

WE GATHER   WE BELIEVE

WE RESPOND

with your family.

We Believe
Family Contract

As a **We Believe** family, this year we promise to

_____

_____

Names

_____

_____

_____

A Family Prayer

Lead your family in prayer.

People who love us make love grow.

Thank you, God, for our family.

People who love us make love grow.

Thank you, God, for all the friends of our family.

Most of all, thank you, God, for loving us!

Look here for connections to the Web and to the Catechism.

Visit Sadlier's

www.WeBelieveweb.com

Connect to the Catechism
References are given here to connect to the *Catechism of the Catholic Church.*

Jesus Christ Is With Us Always

UNIT 1 SHARING FAITH as a Family

Why Children Need to Know Their Family Story

Storytelling comes naturally in most families. This might bring to mind images of children sitting in rapt attention at Granny's feet, but the reality is generally less picturesque. Families tell stories informally and spontaneously, often without realizing it. It is an important part of home life for a number of reasons.

Stories convey a sense of belonging and connect us with something larger than ourselves. This becomes critical as extended families move farther away from one another. Sometimes the only way to "know" a grandparent or cousin is through a story. Children like to hear their own story—about when they were born or baptized, who was there, and how their arrival affected others. It lets them know they hold a unique place in the family.

Storytelling fosters a sense of empathy. Every family has stories of hurt as well as happiness, of failure as well as success. When we talk honestly about our family history, we can more readily understand the difficulties that other families face. In an even broader vein, we ultimately connect with our religious story. We realize how it has affected our whole life. God has been with each of us through good times and bad.

Note the Quote
"Always do right, this will gratify some and astonish the rest."

Mark Twain

From the Catechism
"Parents have the first responsibility for the education of their children."
(Catechism of the Catholic Church, 2223)

What Your Child Will Learn in Unit 1

Unit 1 presents the children with one of the most profound and comforting aspects of our faith: Jesus Christ is with us always. The children will grow in their understanding that Jesus is the Son of God and is the second Person of the Blessed Trinity who became man. They will learn the major events of Jesus' life on earth and appreciate the fact that Jesus Christ gave us the Church. The children will see themselves as part of a celebrating community of believers. They are part of a community that celebrates its living faith through the seven sacraments and meets Jesus in each of the sacraments. The unit concludes with a chapter devoted to the sacrament of Baptism and a chapter fully describing the sacrament of Confirmation.

Plan & Preview

▶ You might want to obtain children's scissors to help your child cut out the beautiful prayer cards on each family page of this unit.

▶ Have available a glass bowl or clear container of water. *(Sharing Faith with My Family, Chapter 4 Family Page)*

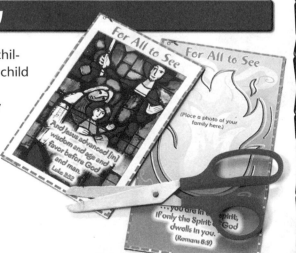

The Language of God

by Mattie Stepanek

Do you know what
Language God speaks?
God speaks Every-Language.
That's because God made
Everyone and gave
Everyone different languages.
And God understands all of them.
And, do you know what is God's
Favorite language?
God's favorite language is
Not grown-up's language,
But the Language of Children.
That's because children
Are special to God.
Children know how to share,
And they never lose
Their Heartsongs.

(Journey through Heartsongs.
Mattie J.T. Stepanek.
New York: VSP Books, Hyperion, 2001.)

Jesus Is the Son of God

✝ We Gather in Prayer

Leader: Let us stand and pray.

Child 1: Glory to the Father,
All: Glory to the Father,

Child 2: and to the Son,
All: and to the Son,

Child 3: and to the Holy Spirit:
All: and to the Holy Spirit:

All: as it was in the
beginning, is now,
and will be for ever.
Amen.

God the Father sent his Son, Jesus, to be with us.

WE GATHER

✝ *God our Father, we thank you.*

Our world is filled with gifts from God. Name some. Why do you think God has given us these gifts?

WE BELIEVE

God the Father loves us very much. He gives us many gifts. He sent his Son, Jesus, to be with us. Jesus is God's greatest gift to us. Jesus is the Son of God.

Mary was a young Jewish girl. God the Father sent an angel to Mary. The angel told her that God chose her to be the mother of his Son. Mary agreed to God's plan. The angel also told her to name the child Jesus. The name *Jesus* has a special meaning. It means "God saves."

After Jesus was born, he lived with his mother, Mary, and his foster father, Joseph. Mary and Joseph cared for Jesus, and they helped him to grow strong. We call Jesus, Mary, and Joseph the **Holy Family**.

Holy Family the family of Jesus, Mary, and Joseph

The Holy Family lived in the town of Nazareth. As Jesus grew, he learned from his family members and teachers about the Jewish faith. He studied the story of God's people. He learned and obeyed God's laws. He prayed and celebrated religious holidays.

WE RESPOND

What do you think Jesus did when he was your age? Act out one thing.

There are many ways we can thank God the Father for sending Jesus. One way is to say the name of Jesus with respect and love.

21

Jesus is human like us.

✝ *Jesus, help us as we learn more about you.*

What do we learn by listening to others?
What do we learn by watching them?

WE BELIEVE

When Jesus was about thirty years old, he left his home town of Nazareth. He began to teach in many towns and villages. Jesus wanted everyone to know that they could share in God's great love. That was the good news Jesus gave to God's people.

Jesus was God's Son but he was also human. People could see Jesus and talk to him. They could reach out to touch him and hear him.

Jesus told them:

- God loves all people.

- God wants all people to love God, to love others, and to love themselves.

- God is their Father.

- God should be the most important one in their lives.

Jesus also taught people by his actions. He fed the hungry. Jesus comforted those who were sad or lonely. He cared for the poor.

Jesus wanted people to know that God always cares for them. Jesus helped people to know that they could always pray to God his Father. Jesus taught the people a prayer that we still pray today.

Discover the name of the prayer. Unscramble the sets of letters. Then write the name to finish the sentence.

U R O

H R A F E T

Jesus taught us

the _____.

As Catholics...

When Jesus taught, he used parables. Parables are short stories. In these stories, Jesus talked about things from everyday life. Some of the things he talked about were flowers, seeds, birds, sheep, and families. The crowds listened carefully to these stories. Jesus used these parables to tell everyone about God's love.

Have you ever heard one of Jesus' parables?

WE RESPOND

Join together to form a circle. Now pray the Our Father together.

How did Jesus show us God's love and care?

Jesus did things only God can do.

WE GATHER

✝ *Jesus, help us to share God's love with others.*

Jesus taught us many things about God the Father. Name one you remember.

WE BELIEVE

Jesus is the Son of God. He did amazing things for people. He showed people that he was divine. **Divine** is a word we use to describe God. This means that Jesus is God and could do things only God can do.

📖 Matthew 8:14–15

One day Jesus visited the family of Peter, one of Jesus' closest friends. "Jesus entered the house of Peter, and saw his mother-in-law lying in bed with a fever. He touched her hand, the fever left her, and she rose and waited on him." (Matthew 8:14–15)

Jesus healed many other people, too. He brought people back to life. He even forgave people their sins.

♫ The words of the following song will tell you about another amazing thing Jesus did. Make up actions for the song. Sing it together.

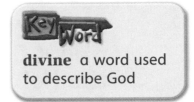
divine a word used to describe God

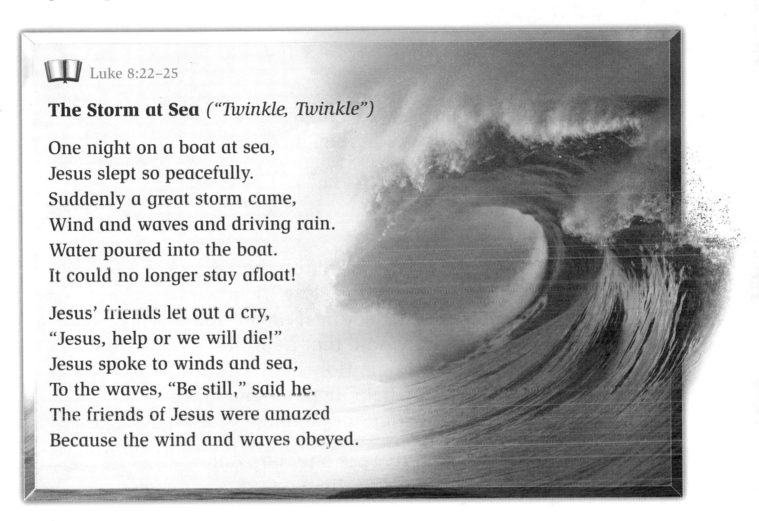

📖 Luke 8:22–25

The Storm at Sea *("Twinkle, Twinkle")*

One night on a boat at sea,
Jesus slept so peacefully.
Suddenly a great storm came,
Wind and waves and driving rain.
Water poured into the boat.
It could no longer stay afloat!

Jesus' friends let out a cry,
"Jesus, help or we will die!"
Jesus spoke to winds and sea,
To the waves, "Be still," said he.
The friends of Jesus were amazed
Because the wind and waves obeyed.

Jesus was able to protect his friends from the storm. This was another sign that Jesus was divine.

WE RESPOND

What would you like to say to Jesus about the wonderful things he did?

Talk to Jesus now about these things. You can do this by praying in the quiet of your heart.

Jesus, the Son of God, taught us about God the Father and God the Holy Spirit.

WE GATHER

✝ *Jesus, we believe that you are the Son of God.*

Think about some things you have been taught. Who helps you to remember these things?

WE BELIEVE

On the night before Jesus died, he shared a very special meal with his close friends. They listened as Jesus told them about God the Father. Then Jesus said that he would ask his Father to send the Holy Spirit. God the Holy Spirit would help them to remember everything that Jesus taught them.

Jesus taught us that there is only one God.
But there are three Persons in one God.
The Father is God.
The Son is God.
The Holy Spirit is God.
We call the three Persons in one God the
Blessed Trinity.

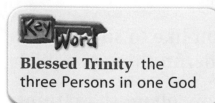

Blessed Trinity the three Persons in one God

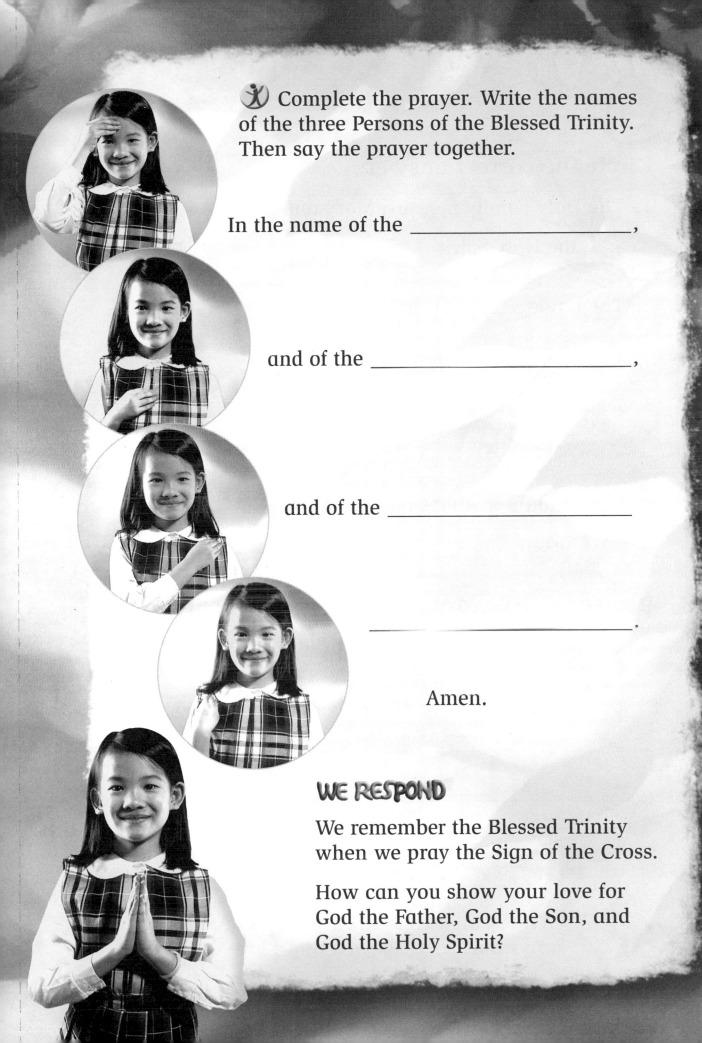

Complete the prayer. Write the names of the three Persons of the Blessed Trinity. Then say the prayer together.

In the name of the _____,

and of the _____,

and of the _____

_____.

Amen.

WE RESPOND

We remember the Blessed Trinity when we pray the Sign of the Cross.

How can you show your love for God the Father, God the Son, and God the Holy Spirit?

Review

Circle the correct answer.

1. The Holy Family is Jesus, Mary and _____ .

2. The name _____ means "God saves."

Jesus   Trinity

3. Jesus brought the _____ that God loves all people.

4. Jesus taught us that God is with us _____ .

Use your own words to complete the sentence.

5. The three Persons in the Blessed Trinity are

ASSESSMENT

Write sentences or draw pictures to tell some ways that Jesus showed God's love.

We Respond in Faith

Reflect & Pray

Jesus wants us to talk to him when we are feeling worried or upset. He also wants us to share with him when we are happy. Write something that you want to tell Jesus.

_____

_____

Key Words

Holy Family (p. 20)
divine (p. 25)
Blessed Trinity (p. 26)

Remember

- God the Father sent his Son, Jesus, to be with us.
- Jesus is human like us.
- Jesus did things only God can do.
- Jesus, the Son of God, taught us about God the Father and God the Holy Spirit.

OUR CATHOLIC LIFE

We Respect All People

God the Father created all people. God wants us to respect every person on earth. Many times it is easy to remember to show respect for those who are older than we are. Sometimes we find it hard to remember to show respect for people who are our age or younger, who speak another language, or who seem different from us.

You can show respect this week by being kind to your classmates. You can help a younger brother, sister, cousin, or neighbor.

SHARING FAITH
with My Family

Sharing What I Learned

Look at the pictures below. Use each picture to tell your family what you learned in this chapter.

For All to See

And Jesus advanced [in] wisdom and age and favor before God and man.
Luke 2:52

A Thank-You Prayer
(Begin and end this prayer with the sign of the cross.)

God, our Father, we thank you for all of the blessings that our family shares.

Jesus, Son of God, thank you for showing us what God is really like.

Holy Spirit, thank you for being with us and guiding us to do the right thing.

Jesus with Us

In the Bible we can read about what Jesus did. Ask each member of your family to share his or her favorite story about Jesus.

Name

_____   _____

_____   _____

Visit Sadlier's
www.WeBelieveweb.com

 Connect to the Catechism
For adult background and reflection, see paragraphs 422, 470, 548, and 243.

Jesus Christ Gives Us the Church

✢ We Gather in Prayer

Leader: Let us take a quiet moment to listen carefully to a story about Jesus.

📖 Matthew 4:18–22

One day Jesus was walking by the sea.
He saw Peter and Andrew catching fish
with a net. Jesus called them, and
asked them to come follow him.
"At once they left their nets and followed him."
(Matthew 4:20)

All: (Clap twice after each line of this response.)

Jesus says to all of us, "Come, follow me."
Come and learn how very happy you can be.
Loving God and loving others,
We are sisters now and brothers.
Jesus says to all of us,
"Come, follow me."

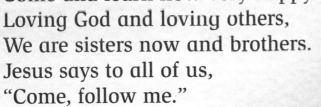

31

Jesus gathered many followers to be his disciples.

WE GATHER

✝ *Jesus, we want to follow you.*

What are some of the good or kind things that teachers do for you? What can you do to be kind to your teachers?

WE BELIEVE

Each day Jesus worked hard as a teacher. He taught people about God the Father's love for them. Jesus showed people how to love God and others. He cared for the sick and the poor. He was good and fair to everyone.

Many people were amazed at the good things Jesus did for others. They began to follow Jesus. Those who followed Jesus were called his **disciples**.

Jesus invited many people to follow him. Peter, Andrew, Mary, and Martha were some of the first disciples of Jesus.

Jesus spent a lot of time with his disciples. He cared about them very much. Jesus helped them to become a community of people who believed in him. They learned from Jesus how to love and to help one another.

From this community, Jesus chose twelve disciples to become its leaders. We call these twelve men the **apostles**.

Jesus Christ asks you to follow him, too! He invites you to be his disciple and friend.

 Are you ready to say yes to the invitation of Jesus? Write your name on the line. Then read the sentence.

_____ is a disciple and friend of Jesus.

WE RESPOND

We are disciples of Jesus when we love God and all people. What are some ways you can show you are a disciple of Jesus?

Remember that a disciple of Jesus prays. Here is a prayer you can say each day.

Here I am, Jesus.
Thank you for inviting me
to follow you.
I love you always! Amen.

Key Words

disciples those who follow Jesus

apostles the twelve men chosen by Jesus to be the leaders of his disciples

Jesus died and rose to new life.

WE GATHER

✝ *Jesus, help us to be your disciples.*

What is a disciple?

Look at the sentences. Circle the ones that tell what a disciple of Jesus would do.

Do homework.   Tell lies.

Be kind.   Help the poor.

Be a bully.   Pray for others.

WE BELIEVE

Jesus tried to share his good news with everyone. Some of the people did not want to follow Jesus. They did not believe in the amazing things Jesus said and did in God's name. There were people who wanted to put Jesus to death.

Jesus was put to death on a cross.

As Catholics...

We celebrate the Resurrection of Jesus Christ at Easter and on every Sunday of the year. At every Mass we remember that Jesus died and rose to new life. Remember this at Mass this week.

After Jesus died, his body was placed in a tomb.

📖 Matthew 28:1–5

Early on Sunday morning, some women disciples of Jesus went to visit the tomb. What a surprise to see an angel sitting in front of the tomb! The angel said to them, "Do not be afraid!" (Matthew 28:5)

The angel told them that Jesus had risen from the dead. Jesus died and rose to new life to save us from sin. Jesus' rising from the dead is called the **Resurrection**. We celebrate Jesus' Resurrection on Easter.

WE RESPOND

🎵 Let us sing Alleluia to show our joy for all Jesus has done for us.

Sing for Joy
Sing and shout for joy, alleluia!
Sing and shout for joy, alleluia!
Sing and shout for joy, alleluia!
Alleluia! Alleluia!

Resurrection Jesus' rising from the dead

How else can you show your happiness that Jesus is risen?

Jesus promised to send the Holy Spirit.

WE GATHER

✢ *Alleluia, Alleluia, Alleluia.*

Do you have a close friend or relative who has moved away? How did you feel when the person first moved?

WE BELIEVE

The risen Jesus visited his disciples before he returned to his Father in heaven. He knew that his disciples would be lonely without him. He wanted them to be close to him always. Jesus promised to send the Holy Spirit to be with his disciples and to help them.

📖 Acts of the Apostles 2:1–4

Early one morning, the disciples were all together in one place. Mary, the mother of Jesus, and some women were there. Suddenly, they heard a noise. It was the sound of a strong wind. Then they saw what looked like flames of fire over each of them. "And they were all filled with the holy Spirit." (Acts of the Apostles 2:4)

Jesus kept his promise. God the Holy Spirit came and would be with the followers of Jesus always.

The Holy Spirit helped the disciples:

• to believe in Jesus
• to be brave in following Jesus
• to love one another
• to teach and help people as Jesus did.

We call the day the Holy Spirit came to help the disciples Pentecost. On Pentecost the Church began. The Church celebrates the feast of Pentecost fifty days after Easter Sunday. During the whole year, we remember that the Holy Spirit is with the Church always.

 Use this code to find an important message.

A B E F G I L N O R V
1 2 3 4 5 6 7 8 9 10 11

The Holy Spirit helps us to be

____ ____ ____ ____ ____ and ____ ____ ____ ____ ____ ____ .
2   10   1   11   3   7   9   11   6   8   5

WE RESPOND

How can the Holy Spirit help you today?

Take a few quiet moments. Ask the Holy Spirit to help you follow Jesus.

37

The Holy Spirit helps the Church to grow.

WE GATHER

✝ *Jesus, thank you for sending the Holy Spirit.*

Think about a time you were very excited about something. You had to tell someone about it! What did you do?

WE BELIEVE

On Pentecost, the disciples of Jesus were very excited. They wanted to tell everyone about Jesus and the Gift of the Holy Spirit.

📖 Acts of the Apostles 2:38–41

On this day Peter and some disciples spoke to a large crowd about the risen Jesus. Peter told them to be baptized and receive the gift of the Holy Spirit.

"Those who accepted his message were baptized, and about three thousand persons were added that day." (Acts of the Apostles 2:41)

The Holy Spirit guided these first members of the Church. They met as a community and prayed together. They helped the sick and the poor. They spread the good news that Jesus had risen.

Since the first Pentecost, the Church has continued to grow. The **Church** is all the people who are baptized in Jesus Christ and follow his teachings.

We are followers of Jesus Christ. We are members of the Church. The Holy Spirit still guides the Church every day. The Holy Spirit helps us to live as Jesus wants us to live. The Holy Spirit helps us to tell others about Jesus Christ.

Church all the people who are baptized in Jesus Christ and follow his teachings

WE RESPOND

How exciting! You can help the Church to grow. You can do this when you do what Jesus taught.

Draw a picture to show one way you can follow Jesus.

Tell someone you know about the good news of Jesus.

Grade 2
Chapter 2

Circle the correct answer.

1. We celebrate Jesus' Resurrection from the dead on _____.

   Pentecost   Easter

2. Those who follow Jesus are his _____.

   fishermen   disciples

3. Jesus died and rose to new life to _____ us.

   save   honor

4. On Pentecost the Church _____.

   ended   began

Use your own words to complete the sentence.

5. The Holy Spirit helps the Church

   _____

   _____

   _____

 Imagine you were in the crowd on the first Pentecost. What did you hear Peter or another disciple say? Write about what you heard.

We Respond in Faith

Reflect & Pray

Disciples of Jesus are kind and fair. They are willing to serve the poor and the weak. They pray and study about Jesus and the Church. What do you find hard to do as a disciple?

Holy Spirit, help me

_____

_____

Key Words

disciples (p. 33)

apostles (p. 33)

Resurrection (p. 35)

Church (p. 39)

Remember

- Jesus gathered many followers to be his disciples.
- Jesus died and rose to new life.
- Jesus promised to send the Holy Spirit.
- The Holy Spirit helps the Church to grow.

OUR CATHOLIC LIFE

Respect for Work

After Pentecost, Jesus' disciples worked hard to spread his message of God's love. They did their best to help the Church grow. The Church teaches that our work is a way to give praise to God. Our work brings about good things in the world. We should appreciate the work every person does.

SHARING FAITH
with My Family

Sharing What I Learned

Look at the pictures below. Use them to tell your family what you learned in this chapter.

For All to See

"They were all filled with the holy Spirit."
(Acts of Apostles 2:4)

Family Echo Prayer

Lead your family in prayer.

For being our teacher,
Thank you, Jesus. (Family Echo)
For giving us new life,
Thank you, Jesus. (Family Echo)
For sending the Holy Spirit,
Thank you, Jesus. (Family Echo)
Amen.

A Family of Disciples

Ask your family what they did this week to show they are followers of Jesus.

Name

_____

_____

What I did this week

_____

_____

Visit Sadlier's

www.WeBelieveweb.com

42

 Connect to the Catechism
For adult background and reflection,
see paragraphs 787, 638, 729, and 737.

We Celebrate God's Love

✝ We Gather in Prayer

Let us stand to pray.

Group 1

"Shout joyfully to the LORD, all you lands;
worship the LORD with cries of gladness;
come before him with joyful song."

Group 2

"Know that the LORD is God,
our maker to whom we belong,
whose people we are."

Groups 1 and 2

"Give thanks to God, bless his name;
good indeed is the LORD,
Whose love endures forever."

Psalm 100:1–3, 4–5

We belong to the Catholic Church.

WE GATHER

✝ *Jesus, we celebrate your love.*

When people work, learn, celebrate, and share with one another in a group, they are a community.

Name some communities to which you belong. Tell what you do together in these groups.

WE BELIEVE

We belong to the Church community that is called the Catholic Church. We are **Catholics**. We become members of the Church when we are baptized. We are led and guided by the pope and bishops.

We worship and work together in communities called **parishes**. Our parish communities are led and guided by priests. They work with men and women of the parish. The whole parish serves the needs of others, especially the poor, sick, and lonely.

Some of the things that Catholics throughout the world share and celebrate are:

- the belief that Jesus is the Son of God
- the belief that Jesus suffered, died, and rose again to save us
- God's life and love
- a call to help and serve others as Jesus did.

WE RESPOND

How do you think others will know that you belong to the Catholic Church?

There are many members of the Catholic Church. But each person is a **VIM**, a **V**ery **I**mportant **M**ember. The Church community needs you to pray, work, and share God's love. Talk to Jesus now about a few ways you can do this.

45

Catholics celebrate God's love by praying and worshiping.

WE GATHER

✝ *Jesus, thank you for giving us the Church.*

What does it mean to celebrate? Think about something you have celebrated. Why were you celebrating? Who was there? What did you say? What did you do?

WE BELIEVE

Jesus and his disciples often shared and celebrated their faith in God. **Faith** is a gift from God. It helps us to trust God and believe all that he tells us.

📖 Mark 11:1, 8–10

The week before Jesus' death and Resurrection, he and his disciples were on their way to Jerusalem. Many people were gathered there to celebrate an important Jewish feast. When people heard that Jesus was coming, many went out to meet him.

Some people spread out their coats on the road. Others cut branches from nearby palm trees. They waved the branches or put them down on the road. The people called out to Jesus with the word *Hosanna.* They called,

"Hosanna!
    Blessed is he who comes in the name
        of the Lord!
Hosanna in the highest!" (Mark 11:9–10)

What did the people do to honor Jesus, the Son of God? What words did they use?

Catholics, too, gather to celebrate God's love. We **worship** God. This means we give him thanks and praise. When we gather to worship, God is with us.

We gather as a parish community each week at Mass. We celebrate all that Jesus has done for us through his life, his death, and his Resurrection. We celebrate that Jesus is with us always. We praise God the Father, through his Son, Jesus Christ, together with the Holy Spirit. God gives us the strength to go out and share his great love.

What are prayerful actions we use to worship God at Mass?

WE RESPOND

When we worship together, we often use this word:

Alleluia

Color in these letters of the word.

What other words can you say to worship God?

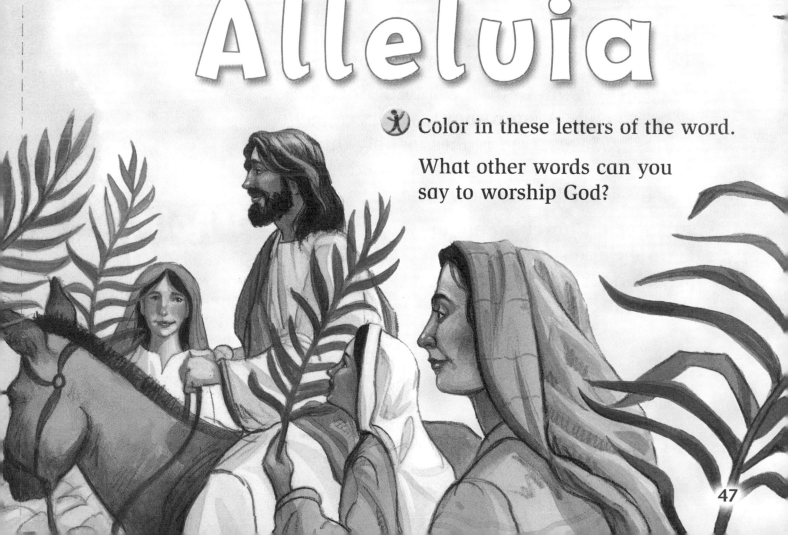

Our Church celebrates with seven special signs called sacraments.

WE GATHER

✝ *Jesus, we offer all that we say and do.*

Here are some signs of celebrations that members of communities enjoy together.

 Draw lines to match each sign with a celebration.

balloon   Fourth of July parade

flag   birthday party

candy heart   Valentine's Day party

WE BELIEVE

The Church celebrates with signs, too. But the signs the Church uses are different from ordinary signs.

The special signs the Church celebrates are the seven sacraments. A **sacrament** is a special sign given to us by Jesus. God makes us holy through the sacraments. Jesus gave us these sacraments so that we can share in God's own life.

We gather as a Church community to celebrate these sacraments. We become stronger in faith. We grow as followers of Jesus.

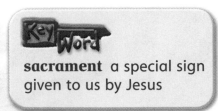

sacrament a special sign given to us by Jesus

As Catholics...

In the Catholic Church, our parish is like our home. Millions of Catholics all around the world gather in their parish communities. In their parishes, Catholics praise and worship God. They celebrate the sacraments. They learn more about their faith. Together they do good works for the people in their communities and in the world.

What is the name of your parish?

WE RESPOND

How would you say thank you to Jesus for giving us the sacraments?
Say it now quietly and prayerfully.

Jesus is present with us in the sacraments.

WE GATHER

✝ *Jesus, we believe that you are with us always.*

Think about times when a friend or a family member was away. What are some things that helped you to remember him or her?

WE BELIEVE

Through God's gift of faith, we believe Jesus is with us. Every time we celebrate the sacraments, Jesus is with us through the power of the Holy Spirit. The sacraments help us to live as friends of Jesus.

Baptism

We become children of God and members of the Church. We receive the Holy Spirit for the first time.

Confirmation

This sacrament seals us with the Gift of the Holy Spirit and strengthens us. Confirmation makes us stronger followers of Jesus.

Eucharist

This is the sacrament of the Body and Blood of Christ. We receive Jesus himself in Holy Communion.

Penance and Reconciliation

In this sacrament, God forgives our sins. We tell our sins to the priest. We are given God's forgiveness and peace.

Anointing of the Sick

This is the sacrament for those who are sick or are in danger of death. The priest prays that they may be healed in body, mind, and spirit.

Matrimony

In this sacrament, a man and a woman become husband and wife. They promise to love and be faithful to each other always.

Holy Orders

In this sacrament, a man becomes a deacon, a priest, or a bishop. He then serves the Church by leading and guiding God's people.

WE RESPOND

Which of the seven sacraments are you looking forward to celebrating this year?

Talk to Jesus about ways you are getting ready to celebrate this sacrament with your parish community.

Circle the correct answer.

1. The Catholic Church celebrates with special signs called _____.

   sacraments   dioceses

2. _____ gave us the sacraments.

   The disciples   Jesus

3. The sacraments give us a share in _____.

   the neighborhood   God's own life

4. There are _____ sacraments.

   three   seven

5. What are some ways Catholics worship?

   _____

   _____

ASSESSMENT Pretend a friend was absent from school this week. Write a sentence to tell your friend what a sacrament is. Then explain some other things you learned about sacraments.

We Respond in Faith

Reflect & Pray

Write to Jesus. Thank him for the sacraments he has given you. Ask him to help you to live out your faith.

_____

_____

_____

Key Words

Catholics (p. 45)

parishes (p. 45)

faith (p. 47)

worship (p. 47)

sacrament (p. 48)

Remember

- We belong to the Catholic Church.
- Catholics celebrate God's love by praying and worshiping.
- Our Church celebrates with seven special signs called sacraments.
- Jesus is present with us in the sacraments.

OUR CATHOLIC LIFE

The Gift of Music

One way we can praise God is through music. The people who play musical instruments and lead us in song help us to praise God at Mass. Some parishes have choirs. We can join with the choir by singing our praise to God.

53

SHARING FAITH
with My Family

Sharing What I Learned

Look at the pictures below. Use each picture to tell your family what you learned in this chapter.

For All to See

"I will sing praise to my God while I live."
(Psalm 104:33)

Gifts from God

Thank God together.

- For our parish community. . . .
- For our parish church where we celebrate the sacraments. . . .
- For sharing with us signs of your love. . . .
- For the gift of meeting Jesus in the seven sacraments. . . .
- For giving us a share in the life of grace. . . .

Signs of Love

Ask the family to tell how each family member is a sign of God's love for that person.

Visit Sadlier's
www.WeBelieveweb.com

 Connect to the Catechism
For adult background and reflection, see paragraphs 1267, 1119, 1123, and 1127.

We Celebrate Baptism

4

✝ We Gather in Prayer

The word *Amen* is a prayer. When we pray this word, we are saying "Yes, we believe!" Let us respond *Amen* together after each of these prayers.

Child 1: God the Father, we believe in you.

Child 2: God the Son, we believe in you.

Child 3: God the Holy Spirit, we believe in you.

All: We arc baptized. We are children of God. We live out the good news of Jesus every day.

At Baptism we become children of God and members of the Church.

WE GATHER

✝ *Amen. Yes, we believe.*

Tell what Pedro told his aunt about Ana's celebration.

> Hi, Aunt Lily! This is Pedro. We're going to have a welcome-to-our-family celebration for Ana. We're going to. . . .

WE BELIEVE

The López family is very happy! They have just welcomed a new baby into their family. The baby's name is Ana.

Soon Ana will belong to another family, the Catholic Church. In Baptism Ana will become a child of God and a member of the Church. When we were baptized, we became children of God and members of the Church, too.

Ana's parents want her to be baptized. They want her to belong to Jesus and to the Church community. Everyone in Ana's family is looking forward to bringing the newest member of their family to the parish church for Baptism.

WE RESPOND

How wonderful that your family brought you to the Church to be baptized. What do you want to say to them?

Baptism is the first sacrament you receive. At your Baptism, your parish welcomed you as a new member of the Church.

Many things happened for you at your Baptism. Write your name on each line on the membership card to remember two important things. Then read the sentences.

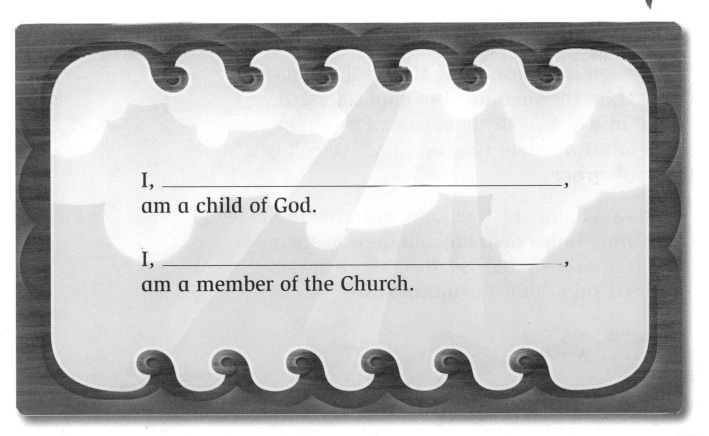

I, _____,
am a child of God.

I, _____,
am a member of the Church.

At Baptism we receive grace, a share in God's life.

WE GATHER

✝ *God the Father, thank you for helping us to grow.*

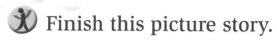 Finish this picture story.

Why is water important in the story?
Why is water important in our lives?

WE BELIEVE

Water is an important sign of the sacrament of Baptism. In the sacrament of Baptism, we are placed in water or water is poured over our foreheads. God gives us a new life. We call God's life in us **grace**.

When God made the first man and woman, he let them share in his own life. But they disobeyed God. They sinned and lost their share in God's life. That first sin is called **original sin**.

We are all born with original sin. Through Baptism, original sin and all other sins are taken away. **Baptism** is the sacrament in which we are freed from sin and given grace, a share in God's life.

WE RESPOND

Why is water a sign of our Baptism?

Close your eyes. Feel cool water pouring over you. Thank God for the gift of grace.

 Make up a tune or a special rhythm for this verse.

God's Life

When we were baptized,
we became your children.
Now we share in your life,
the life of grace.
We know you love us.
Help us grow in your love.
Thank you, God, for sharing
your life of grace with us.

We celebrate the sacrament of Baptism with special words and actions.

WE GATHER

✝ *God, help us grow in your love.*

Do you remember learning to pray the Sign of the Cross? Who taught you?

WE BELIEVE

This is what happened when the López family and their friends celebrated Ana's Baptism.

- Father Ramón and the parish community greeted the family.

- Father told Ana's parents and godparents that they should help Ana to keep growing in faith.

- Father traced the sign of the cross on Ana's forehead. Ana's parents and godparents did this also. This action showed that Ana now belonged to Jesus in a special way.

- Father Ramón read a story about Jesus. Father talked about the story.

- Father blessed the water in the baptismal pool.

- Father asked Ana's parents and godparents if they reject sin. He asked them if they believe in God the Father, God the Son, and God the Holy Spirit. Everyone answered, "I do" to all the questions.

- Father placed Ana in the water of the baptismal pool three times. He said the words of Baptism. It was with water and these words that Ana was baptized:

Ana, I baptize you in the name
  of the Father,
and of the Son,
and of the Holy Spirit.

Each of us was baptized with water and these same words.

WE RESPOND

Pray together these words:

O God, we thank you for our families, our godparents, and parish community. May we help each other to keep growing in your love.

Who do you think was at your Baptism? Ask your family to tell you.

We can show that we are children of God by what we say and do.

WE GATHER

✝ *Pray the Our Father together.*

Do you belong to a club or a team? What actions show others that you are a member?

WE BELIEVE

The following words and actions were also a part of the celebration of Ana's Baptism in her parish.

- Father Ramón put a white garment on Ana. He said that the white garment showed that Ana was a friend and follower of Jesus.

- Ana's godmother went to the large Easter candle by the baptismal pool. She lit a smaller candle for Ana from it. Father told Ana's parents and godparents to help keep the light of Christ burning in Ana's life.

- Father Ramón invited everyone to pray the Our Father together.

- Father blessed the family and everyone in church.

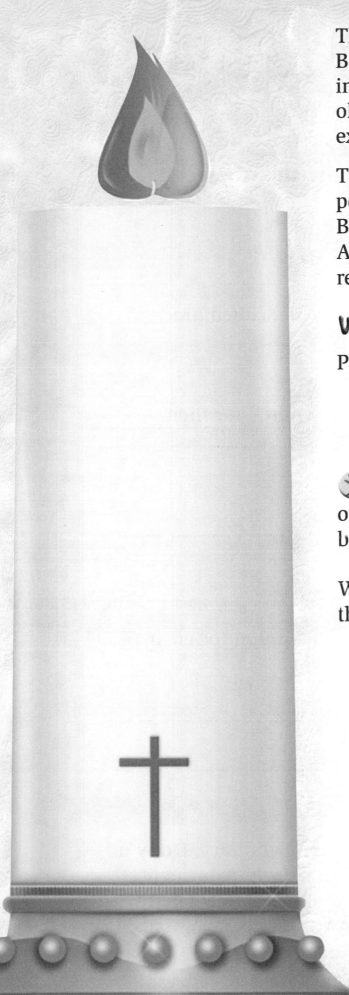

The López family will keep Ana's Baptism candle and white garment in a special place. When Ana is older, her family can use these to explain her Baptism to her.

These same words and actions were part of the celebration of your Baptism. Talk with your family. Ask them to share what they remember about your celebration.

WE RESPOND

Pray together.

> Jesus, we believe that you are the Light of the World. Help us to share your light with others.

On the candle write the names of people who are helping you to become a good Catholic.

What will you do and say to share the light of Christ with others?

As Catholics...

Godmothers and godfathers are very special people. They are chosen by the parents of the child being baptized. They have a special role in this sacrament. They agree to help the parents teach the child about their Catholic faith. The godparents help the child to live as a friend of Jesus. They help the child to love God and others.

How can you say thank you to your godparents?

Circle the correct answer.
Circle ? if you do not know the answer.

1. Water is a sign of Baptism.

    Yes   No   ?

2. At Baptism we receive God's life, called grace.

    Yes   No   ?

3. Parents are the only ones in church for their child's Baptism.

    Yes   No   ?

4. We are all born with original sin.

    Yes   No   ?

5. Why is Baptism a special celebration for each one of us?

    _____

    _____

Make a Baptism picture dictionary. Draw a picture of a candle, cross, white garment, baptismal pool or font, and water. Then write a sentence to tell how each thing is used in Baptism.

We Respond in Faith

Reflect & Pray

Talk to Jesus about Baptism. Write one or two things you can do to show that you are a child of God.

_____

_____

Key Words

grace (p. 59)
original sin (p. 59)
Baptism (p. 59)

Remember

• At Baptism we become children of God and members of the Church.

• At Baptism we receive grace, a share in God's life.

• We celebrate the sacrament of Baptism with special words and actions.

• We can show that we are children of God by what we say and do.

OUR CATHOLIC LIFE

Preparing for Baptism

Most Catholics are baptized as infants. In parishes there is a special group of people who meet to help the children's families prepare for their child's Baptism. Many times a priest or deacon and other parents are in this group. This group talks about Baptism and what it means. They also talk about the words and actions used to celebrate the sacrament. Baptism is celebrated with the parish community, often at Sunday Mass. The parish community welcomes the new members and promises to help them live as faithful followers of Jesus.

SHARING FAITH
with My Family

Sharing What I Learned

Look at the pictures below. Use each picture to tell your family what you learned in this chapter.

For All to See

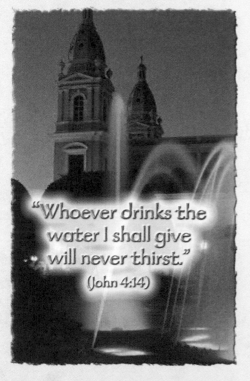

"Whoever drinks the water I shall give will never thirst."
(John 4:14)

We Say "I Do"

(Place a bowl of water in the middle of the table.)

Child: Do you believe in God the Father, Jesus Christ, his Son, and the Holy Spirit, Giver of Life?

All: I do. (Trace the sign of the cross on the forehead of the person next to you.)

Child: Do you believe that Jesus Christ saves us?

All: I do. (Dip your fingers in the bowl of water.)

Child: O God, we thank you for the gift of Baptism. We are members of your Church. We believe in you and we praise you.

All: Amen.

Let's Talk Ask the members of the family to share what they know about their Baptism celebrations.

Visit Sadlier's
www.WEBELIEVEweb.com

 Connect to the Catechism
For adult background and reflection, see paragraphs 1213, 1250, 1234, and 1265.

We Celebrate Confirmation

5

✝ We Gather in Prayer

Close your eyes. Be very still.
Breathe in. Breathe out.
Try to feel God's love around you.

Join hands and form a prayer circle.
Pray the following words:

> Come, Holy Spirit,
> fill the hearts of your
> faithful people
> and kindle in us
> the fire of your love.

We celebrate the Gift of the Holy Spirit in the sacrament of Confirmation.

WE GATHER

✝ *Come, Holy Spirit.*

Do you remember what happened at Pentecost? Where were the disciples? What did they see on that day? What changed them?

 Act out the story together.

WE BELIEVE

Jesus promised to send the Holy Spirit to the apostles and other disciples to be their helper. The Holy Spirit made them strong and brave followers of Jesus. The Holy Spirit helped the disciples to remember everything Jesus had said and done.

The Holy Spirit filled the disciples with courage and faith. They began to tell everyone about Jesus. The disciples told everyone Jesus died for us and rose to new life.

The apostles baptized many people. They laid their hands on people so that they too might receive the Holy Spirit. They prayed for the new members of the Church. They wanted them to be strong in faith and to care for one another's needs.

The Holy Spirit is God, the third Person of the Blessed Trinity. The Holy Spirit was sent by the Father and Jesus to help and guide the Church. The Holy Spirit is still with us today. We celebrate the Gift of the Holy Spirit in the sacrament of Confirmation.

The Church often uses a picture of fire or a flame to remind us of the Holy Spirit. Fire gives us light, warmth, and energy. The Holy Spirit helps us

- to follow Jesus Christ, the Light of the World
- to know the warmth of God's love and to share it with others
- to have energy to share God's love, even when it is difficult for us.

WE RESPOND

Name one way the Holy Spirit can help you.

 Complete this prayer.

God the Holy Spirit, help me to _____

_____

_____

Confirmation seals us with the Gift of the Holy Spirit and strengthens us.

WE GATHER

✝ *Holy Spirit, we believe that you are with us.*

Circle the correct answers.

During gym class, you make your muscles_____.

weak   firm

Another word for firm is_____.

strong   late

What do you think *to confirm* means?

WE BELIEVE

The sacraments of Baptism and Confirmation are like partners. Baptism makes us children of God and members of the Church. Each of us received the Holy Spirit when we were baptized. **Confirmation** is the sacrament that seals us with the Gift of the Holy Spirit and strengthens us. The Holy Spirit helps us to be strong followers of Jesus. We show that we follow Jesus by the way we live.

The parish community prays for the people about to be confirmed. The community gathers with them for the celebration of the sacrament.

Most often a bishop comes to the parish to confirm people. Sometimes the bishop appoints a priest to do the confirming. The sacrament of Confirmation is celebrated during Mass, after the gospel is read and explained.

Confirmation the sacrament that seals us with the Gift of the Holy Spirit and strengthens us

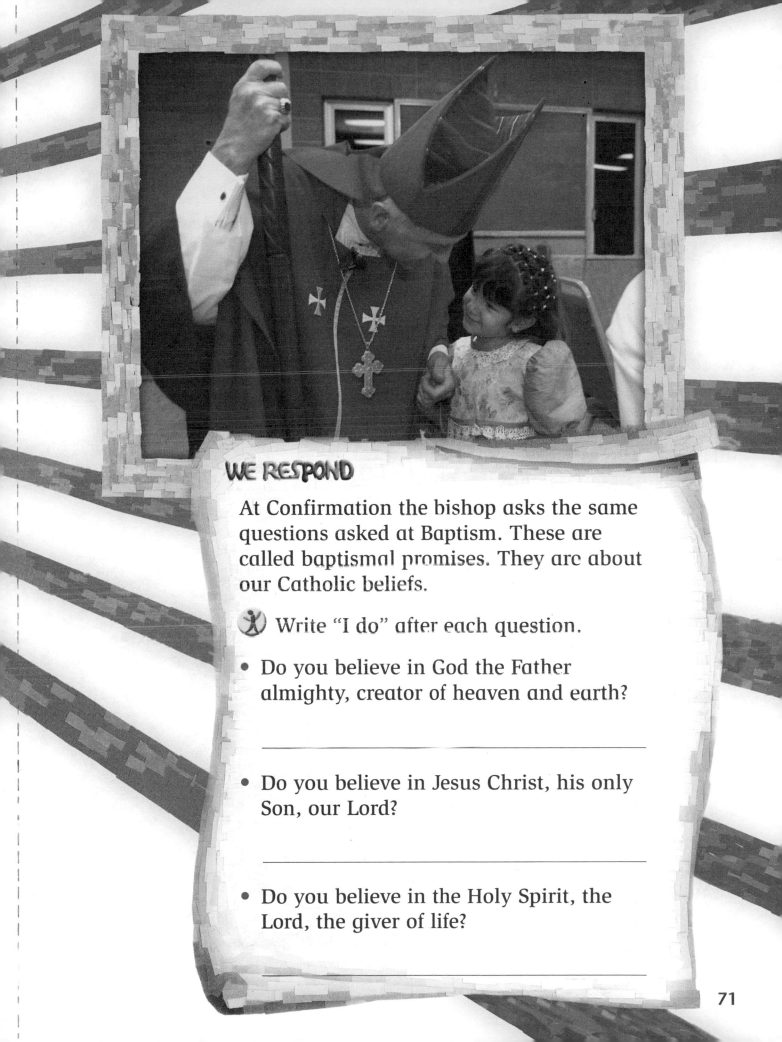

WE RESPOND

At Confirmation the bishop asks the same questions asked at Baptism. These are called baptismal promises. They are about our Catholic beliefs.

Write "I do" after each question.

- Do you believe in God the Father almighty, creator of heaven and earth?

_____

- Do you believe in Jesus Christ, his only Son, our Lord?

_____

- Do you believe in the Holy Spirit, the Lord, the giver of life?

_____

We celebrate the sacrament of Confirmation with special words and actions.

WE GATHER

✝ *Holy Spirit, be our Helper and our Guide.*

What kinds of oil do we use in our homes?

WE BELIEVE

In the time of Jesus, the leaders of God's people were anointed with oil. This action showed that these leaders were set apart to do God's work. God was with the leaders in a special way.

At Confirmation we are anointed with oil. This shows that we are set apart to do God's work. The anointing with oil shows that the Holy Spirit is with us. A person called a sponsor helps us as we get ready for Confirmation.

This is what happens during Confirmation.

- The bishop talks with the people about their faith. He calls them to live their lives in service for all. Sometimes he asks them questions, too.

- The bishop and priests who are present stretch out their hands over those receiving the sacrament. The bishop prays that the Holy Spirit will strengthen these people with special gifts.

- The bishop dips his right thumb in blessed oil. Laying his hand on the person's head, he traces a cross on that person's forehead with the oil. We call tracing the cross with oil the **anointing with oil**.

The bishop prays, "(Person's name), be sealed with the Gift of the Holy Spirit."

The person responds, "Amen." Then the bishop says, "Peace be with you." Those who were confirmed say, "And also with you."

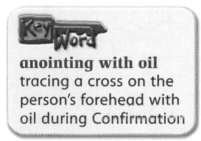

anointing with oil tracing a cross on the person's forehead with oil during Confirmation

WE RESPOND

🎵 **Make Us Strong**
(*"My Darling Clementine"*)

Holy Spirit, Holy Spirit,
Holy Spirit, make us strong,
So that we can follow Jesus
And bring God's love to everyone.

🏃 Make up actions for this song.

How can you show that the Holy Spirit is with you?

As Catholics...

The week before Easter is called Holy Week. Each year during Holy Week, the bishop blesses three oils of the Church. The oils are given to all the parishes that make up the diocese. One blessed oil is called *Chrism*. It is used for anointing in the sacraments of Baptism, Confirmation, and Holy Orders.

When were you anointed with Chrism?

The Holy Spirit helps baptized Catholics and confirmed Catholics.

WE GATHER

✝ *Holy Spirit, stay with us always.*

Are there people in your family, school, and community who help you to learn and grow in your faith? Who are they? How do they help you?

WE BELIEVE

The Holy Spirit helps Catholics who have been baptized and Catholics who have been confirmed to do the following things.

- Love God and others as Jesus taught.
- Worship God and celebrate the sacraments.
- Treat others with respect.
- Care for those who are poor, hungry, or sick.
- Be fair.
- Be peacemakers.
- Be happy with all that God has given them.
- Live out their faith.
- Stand up for what they believe.

Look at the pictures on these pages. For each write how the Holy Spirit is helping the people live as baptized and confirmed Catholics.

_____

_____

_____

_____

WE RESPOND

Which actions listed or shown on these two pages are easy for you to do? Which are difficult?

Talk to the Holy Spirit about these ways. Ask for help with the actions that are difficult.

Circle the correct answer.

1. The sacrament of _____ seals us with the Gift of the Holy Spirit.

   Matrimony   Confirmation

2. At Confirmation the bishop or priest traces a cross with blessed _____ on a person's forehead.

   water   oil

3. The Church uses _____ to remind us of the Holy Spirit.

   fire   a white garment

4. Confirmation calls us to _____ .

   live out our faith   be selfish

5. What are some ways the Holy Spirit helps baptized and confirmed Catholics?

   _____

   _____

ASSESSMENT

With a partner act out what happens at Confirmation. Then write sentences about what happens.

We Respond in Faith

Reflect & Pray

Write your own prayer to the Holy Spirit.

_____

_____

_____

Key Words

Confirmation (p. 70)

anointing with oil (p. 73)

Remember

- We celebrate the Gift of the Holy Spirit in the sacrament of Confirmation.
- Confirmation seals us with the Gift of the Holy Spirit and strengthens us.
- We celebrate the sacrament of Confirmation with special words and actions.
- The Holy Spirit helps baptized Catholics and confirmed Catholics.

OUR CATHOLIC LIFE

Helping Those in Need

Floods, fires, or other disasters can leave people homeless. Many Catholic parishes open their halls and school gyms as shelters. People in the parishes volunteer and bring water, food, and clothing for these people. They also bring toys and books for the children.

Catholics continue to work to help these people who have suffered from these disasters.

SHARING FAITH
with My Family

Sharing What I Learned

Look at the pictures below. Use each picture to tell your family what you learned in this chapter.

For All to See

(Place a photo of your family here.)

"You are in the spirit, if only the Spirit of God dwells in you."
(Romans 8:9)

Calling on the Holy Spirit

(Each member of the family completes one of the following petitions.)

Holy Spirit, give us the courage to

_____.

Holy Spirit, help us to love

_____.

Child: Peace be with you.

All: And also with you.

Spirit Alive

Ask each member of the family to share how the Holy Spirit is helping them each day. How can you remind each other that this is true?

Visit Sadlier's
www.WeBelieveweb.com

 Connect to the Catechism
For adult background and reflection, see paragraphs 1285, 1295, 1299, and 1303.

The Church Year

Advent Christmas Ordinary Time Lent Three Days Easter Ordinary Time

Jesus said, "Follow me."

Mark 2:14

The Church year helps us to follow Jesus.

WE GATHER

What does it mean to follow Jesus? Name some ways you follow Jesus.

WE BELIEVE

All during the year, we gather with our parish to worship. Together we celebrate the Eucharist and the other sacraments.

The Church year is made up of special times called seasons. During the different seasons, we grow in love for Jesus. We grow as his followers.

Advent is a season of waiting and preparing. We wait and get ready for the coming of the Son of God.

Christmas is a time to celebrate the birth of the Son of God. We rejoice that Jesus is with us always.

Lent is a season of preparing. We remember all that Jesus did to save us. We get ready for the Church's greatest celebration.

The Three Days are the Church's greatest celebration. We celebrate Jesus' death and Resurrection.

Easter is a time of great joy. We rejoice and celebrate that Jesus rose to new life.

Ordinary Time is when we celebrate everything about Jesus, especially his life and teachings.

Advent

Christmas

Ordinary Time

Lent

Three Days

Easter

Ordinary Time

The seasons of the Church year help us to follow Jesus. We want to grow closer to Jesus. He is God's greatest gift to us. Jesus loves us and gives us life. He is always with us. He is here, today and every day.

WE RESPOND

Each season of the Church year has a special color. Color the Church year time line to follow Jesus through the seasons. On the lines write, "Jesus, I will follow you." Then put an X on the part of the time line to show the season you are celebrating now.

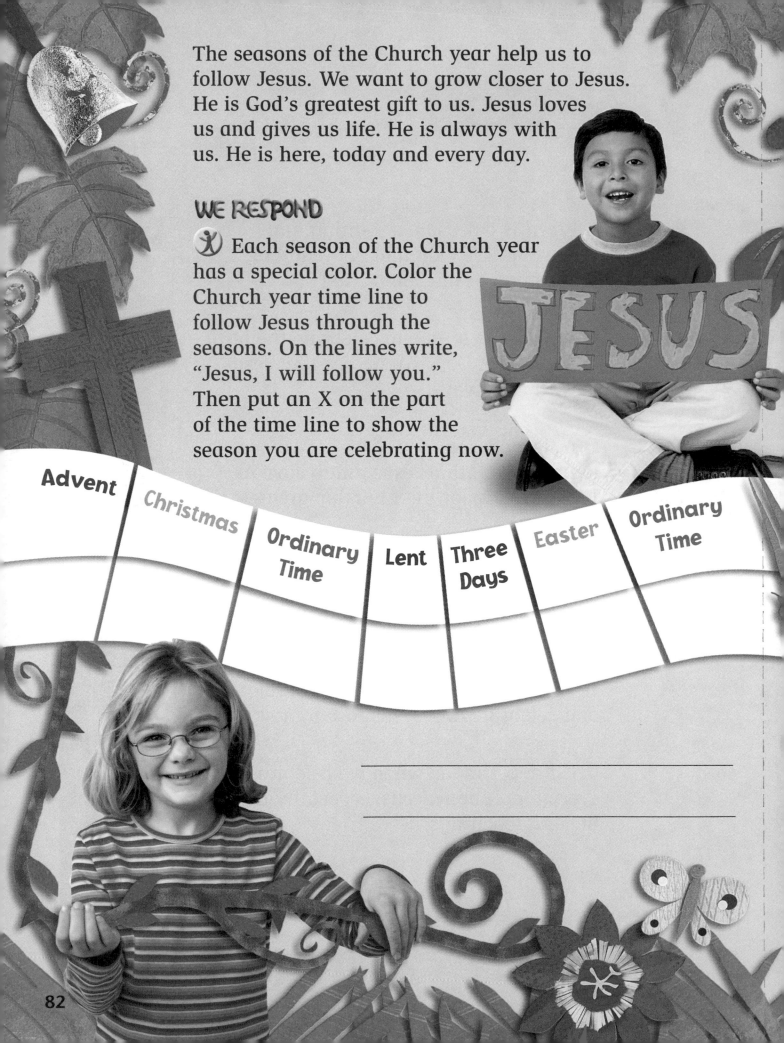

Advent   Christmas   Ordinary Time   Lent   Three Days   Easter   Ordinary Time

_____

_____

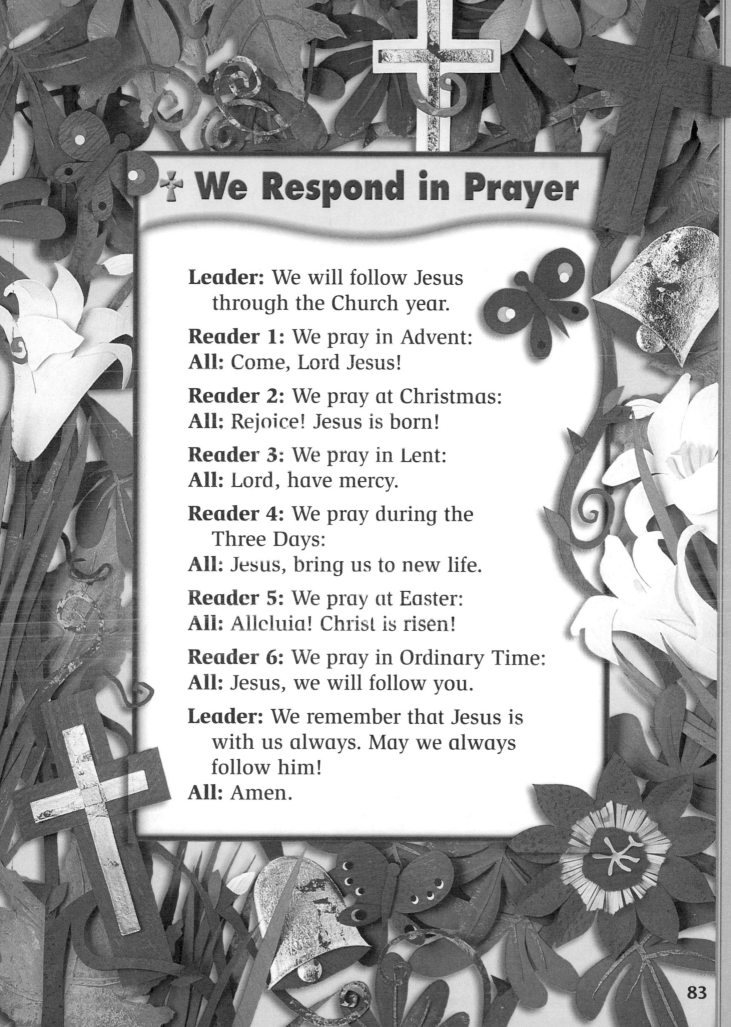

✝ We Respond in Prayer

Leader: We will follow Jesus through the Church year.

Reader 1: We pray in Advent:
All: Come, Lord Jesus!

Reader 2: We pray at Christmas:
All: Rejoice! Jesus is born!

Reader 3: We pray in Lent:
All: Lord, have mercy.

Reader 4: We pray during the Three Days:
All: Jesus, bring us to new life.

Reader 5: We pray at Easter:
All: Alleluia! Christ is risen!

Reader 6: We pray in Ordinary Time:
All: Jesus, we will follow you.

Leader: We remember that Jesus is with us always. May we always follow him!
All: Amen.

THE CHURCH YEAR

SHARING FAITH
with My Family

Sharing What I Learned

Look at the pictures below. Use them to tell your family what you learned in this chapter.

A Family Prayer to Follow Jesus

May the peace of Christ rule in our hearts, and may the word of Christ in all its richness dwell in us, so that whatever we do in word and in work, we will do in the name of the Lord. Amen.

Around the Table

Show your family the Church year chart on page 81. Show them the season we are celebrating now. Tell what season comes next. Talk about what your family can do at home to celebrate this season or to prepare for the next one. How can you share this season with an elderly person or someone who lives alone?

Visit Sadlier's

www.WeBelieveweb.com

Connect to the Catechism
For adult background and reflection, see paragraph 1168.

Ordinary Time

Advent | Christmas | Ordinary Time | Lent | Three Days | Easter | Ordinary Time

"Every day I will bless you;
I will praise your name forever."

Psalm 145:2

85

In Ordinary Time, we celebrate Jesus Christ and learn to follow him.

WE GATHER

What are some things that you put in order? How do you put them in order?

WE BELIEVE

What do we celebrate in Ordinary Time? We celebrate Jesus Christ! We do not remember only one event of his life. We remember and learn about his whole life, death, and Resurrection. We celebrate Jesus Christ and everything about him!

Jesus teaches the disciples to pray, "Our Father." (Matthew 6:9)

This season is called Ordinary Time because the Church puts the Sundays in number order.

The season of Ordinary Time comes twice each year. It comes between the seasons of Christmas and Lent. Ordinary Time comes again between the Easter season and the season of Advent. The special color of Ordinary Time is green.

During Ordinary Time we:

- learn more about Jesus
- listen to his teachings read from the Bible
- learn how to follow Jesus in our everyday lives.

Look at the pictures on these pages. What does each one show you about Jesus? What does each one show about his teachings?

Jesus calls us. He says, "Let the children come to me." (Matthew 19:14)

All through the year, the most special day of the week is Sunday. Jesus rose from the dead on a Sunday.

On Sundays we gather with our parish to celebrate Mass. We listen to the word of God and receive the Eucharist. Every Sunday, we learn more about Jesus and grow closer to him. We rest from work. We spend time with family and friends.

WE RESPOND

Draw a picture to show what your family can do on Sundays in Ordinary Time.

✠ We Respond in Prayer

Leader: In Ordinary Time, we also celebrate special days in honor of Mary, the mother of Jesus and our mother. One of these days is the feast of Our Lady of the Rosary on October 7.

Side 1: Hail Mary, full of grace,
the Lord is with you!
Blessed are you among women, and
blessed is the fruit of your womb, Jesus.

Side 2: Holy Mary, Mother of God,
pray for us sinners,
now and at the hour of our death.

All: Amen.

Leader: Glory to the Father, and to the Son, and to the Holy Spirit:

All: As it was in the beginning, is now, and will be for ever. Amen.

🎵 **Yes, We Will Do What Jesus Says**

Mary said, "Do what Jesus tells you."
Mary said, "Do what Jesus says."
Yes, we will do what Jesus tells us,
yes, we will do what Jesus says.

ORDINARY TIME

SHARING FAITH
with My Family

Sharing What I Learned

Look at the pictures below. Use them to tell your family what you learned in this chapter.

A Family Prayer on Sunday Evening

On Sunday evening before going to bed, ask your family to say this prayer together:

God, we thank you for the joy and rest of this day.

A Sign for Mary

Here is a sign for Mary. The M stands for Mary and for mother. There is a cross in the M. This reminds us that we honor Mary because she is the mother of Jesus.

Color this sign. Then be on the lookout for other places where you can find this sign.

Visit Sadlier's

www.WeBelieveweb.com

Connect to the Catechism
For adult background and reflection, see paragraph 1173.

Fill in the circle next to the correct answer.

1. Jesus, Mary, and Joseph are called the _____.

   ○ Trinity   ○ Holy Family   ○ Church

2. At Baptism we receive God's life, called _____.

   ○ cross   ○ grace   ○ holy

3. The Church celebrates with special signs called _____.

   ○ grace   ○ apostles   ○ sacraments

4. Confirmation calls us to _____.

   ○ live our faith   ○ be selfish   ○ be quiet

5. God the Father sent his Son, Jesus, to be with us.

   ○ Yes   ○ No

6. There are ten sacraments.

   ○ Yes   ○ No

7. Jesus promised to send the Holy Spirit to help his followers.

   ○ Yes   ○ No

8. On Christmas we celebrate the coming of the Holy Spirit.

   ○ Yes   ○ No

continued on next page

Tell what you know about:

9. Easter Sunday

10. the Blessed Trinity

ALTERNATIVE ASSESSMENT

Use a blue crayon to circle the words about Baptism. Use a red crayon to circle the words about Confirmation.

water

bishop

become a member of the Church

pool or font

original sin taken away

laying on of hands

sealed with the Gift of the Holy Spirit

Choose one of these projects. Do your work on a separate piece of paper.

• Imagine you are Peter or one of the other disciples of Jesus. Write a letter home. Tell your family about things Jesus has said and done.

• Draw a picture to show one way Jesus shared God's love. Talk about your picture.

Jesus Calls Us to Penance and Reconciliation

UNIT
2

UNIT 2 SHARING FAITH as a Family

What the Church Can Teach Families About Forgiveness

The way in which the Church understands Reconciliation can be a helpful model for families to follow. It is primarily a three-step process:

We must first experience a change of heart. In religious terms, this is called *conversion*. It means coming to a realization, either on our own or with the help of another, that what we have done or said is hurtful and we regret it. Because this must come from the heart, it never works when someone forces us to apologize.

Secondly, we need to express this in some way—usually to the person we have hurt. *Confession* is good for the soul because it allows us to let go of what troubles us. We do this with words and gestures that say in some way, "I'm sorry. I love you. I want this disagreement to end."

Genuine remorse brings us, in the end, to a *resolution* so that the same patterns don't repeat themselves. We might change the way we communicate so that our words are not misunderstood. It might mean being more attentive to stressful situations that cause us to snap at one another.

No family is going to live in perfect harmony. Forgiveness is a practice that helps us heal and move on.

Note the Quote
"For the things we have to learn before we can do them, we learn by doing them."

Aristotle

From the Catechism
"The relationships within the family bring an affinity of feelings, affections and interests, arising above all from the members' respect for one another."
(Catechism of the Catholic Church, 2206)

What Your Child Will Learn in Unit 2

In this unit, the children will feel Jesus' call to peace and reconciliation. They will grasp more fully the importance of listening to the word of God as found in the Old Testament and the New Testament. Leading from this is a chapter devoted to explaining the Ten Commandments and the Great Commandment. The children will appreciate that true freedom comes from following God's laws. Making bad choices and turning away from God's love is discussed in the context of Jesus' promise to give us his forgiveness. God always loves us and shows us mercy. A large part of this unit (two chapters) is devoted to the sacrament of Penance and Reconciliation.

Plan & Preview

► You might want to obtain children's scissors to help your child cut out the beautiful prayer cards on each family page of this unit.

► If you have a family Bible, make it available for sharing with your child. *(Chapters 8 & 10 Family Pages)*

► Obtain a large sheet of drawing or butcher paper as well as some markers or crayons. *(Chapter 9 Family Page)*

Bible Q & A

Q: Where can I find stories about forgiveness?
-Seattle, Washington

A: Forgiveness was one of Jesus' major themes. For stories that illustrate forgiveness, read Matthew 18:21-35 and Luke 15:11-32.

Did You Know?

In a recent survey, people were asked: Are you a member of a church or synagogue?

64% answered yes

36% answered no

(Most Recent Church Membership Trend, Mar 18–20, 2002, The Gallup Organization)

We Learn About God's Love

✝ We Gather in Prayer

Leader: Let us gather to listen to God's word.

Reader: God said,
"I, the LORD, your God,
teach you what is for
   your good,
and lead you on the way
   you should go."
(Isaiah 48:17)

Leader: Oh God, we want to understand your word.

All: God, help us to remember all the good things you teach us. Help us to follow your ways of love.

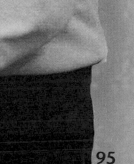

The Bible is the book of God's word.

✝ *God, we believe you are with us.*

What kind of books do you like?
What are these books about?

WE BELIEVE

God has always wanted us to
know and love him. He wants
us to tell others about him, too.

Long ago the Holy Spirit helped
certain people to write about God's
love. Different writers wrote in
different ways. Some wrote stories.
Some wrote poems. Some wrote
wise sayings. Others wrote about
interesting people and events.

These writings were put into one large
book called the Bible. The Bible has
seventy-three smaller books in it.

God the Holy Spirit guided the people
who wrote the Bible. So the **Bible** is the
book in which God's word is written.

As Catholics...

We also call the Bible Sacred
Scripture. The word *sacred* means
"holy." The word *Scripture* comes
from a word that means "writings."

We keep the Bible in a special
place in our homes and churches.
Together make a special place in
your classroom for the Bible.

When we read the Bible, we learn:

- what God has told us about himself and his love
- what God wants us to do to live as his children.

WE RESPOND

The Bible is the most important book of all time. Why do you think this is true?

Draw a cover for the Bible. It should show that the Bible is a very special book about God.

Key Word

Bible the book in which God's word is written

The Old Testament is the first part of the Bible.

WE GATHER

✝ *O God, thank you for speaking your word to us.*

How do you learn about people who lived long ago?

Circle your favorite ways.

read books	watch movies
listen to stories	go to museums
check the Internet	listen to songs

WE BELIEVE

The Bible has two parts. The first part is called the **Old Testament.** In this part we learn about God's people who lived before Jesus' time on earth. We read about the many wonderful things God did for his people. We read about the ways God showed special love for them. We also learn how they showed their love for God.

In the Old Testament we learn about the lives of many people. One of the people we read about is David. When David was young, he was a shepherd. He took care of sheep near the town of Bethlehem.

God was pleased with David. God loved him very much. David was chosen by God to become king.

David showed his great love for God by praising him. David said, "Great are you, Lord GOD!" (2 Samuel 7:22)

WE RESPOND

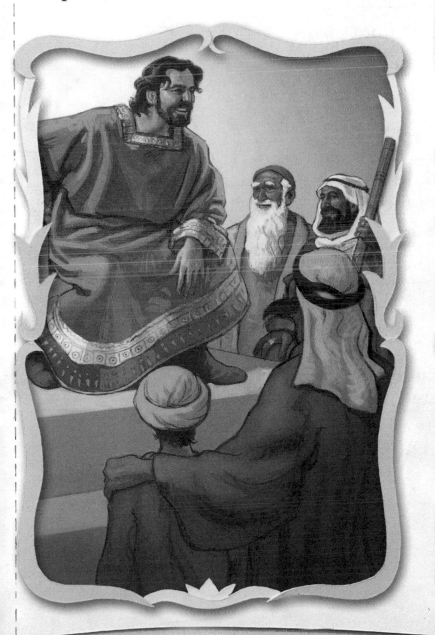 There are many ways to praise God. Share the words and actions you use to praise God.

The New Testament is the second part of the Bible.

WE GATHER

✝ *God, thank you for all those who tell us about your love.*

🏃 Imagine you have just heard good news. You heard that the new playground opened today. Show what you would do to share this good news.

WE BELIEVE

In Jesus' time, some people traveled from town to town to tell people what was happening.

📖 Luke 4:42–43

One morning a crowd went to see Jesus. They tried to stop him from leaving their town. But Jesus said, "To the other towns also I must proclaim the good news of the kingdom of God, because for this purpose I have been sent." (Luke 4:43)

This reading is from the second part of the Bible. The second part of the Bible is the **New Testament**. The New Testament is about Jesus Christ and his disciples. It is also about the beginning of the Church.

Four of the books in the New Testament are called the **gospels**. They are very special. They are about Jesus' teachings and his life on earth.

The word *gospel* means "good news." Every word and action of Jesus is good news for us. We learn the good news of Jesus Christ in the gospels.

- God is our Father who loves and forgives us.

- Jesus is with us always. He teaches us how to love and do good.

- The Holy Spirit helps us and guides us.

New Testament the second part of the Bible

gospels four of the books in the New Testament that are about Jesus' teachings and his life on earth

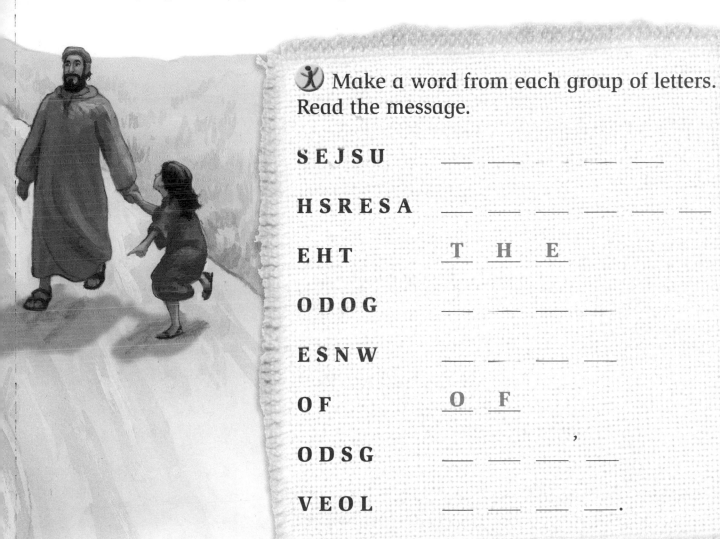

Make a word from each group of letters. Read the message.

SEJSU   ___ ___ ___ ___ ___

HSRESA   ___ ___ ___ ___ ___ ___

EHT   T H E

ODOG   ___ ___ ___ ___

ESNW   ___ ___ ___ ___

OF   O F

ODSG   ___ ___ ___ '___

VEOL   ___ ___ ___ ___.

WE RESPOND

When and where have you heard stories about Jesus? What is your favorite story about him?

Jesus wants us to listen to his teachings.

WE GATHER

✝ *Jesus, we will share your good news.*

Imagine you are having a fire drill in school. Why does your teacher tell you to listen carefully to the directions?

WE BELIEVE

Jesus told us that it is very important to listen to his teachings. One day Jesus had been teaching for a long time. Jesus had taught people about believing in God and praying to him. Jesus ended by telling this story.

Matthew 7:24–27

A man built his house on rock. When storms came, the wind blew. The rain beat against the house. But the house did not fall. It had been built on rock.

Jesus told the people, "Everyone who listens to these words of mine and acts on them will be like a wise man who built his house on rock." (Matthew 7:24)

When we listen to God's word in the Bible, we hear with our ears. We remember in our minds and hearts. We show we have listened by loving God and helping others.

 Look at the pictures.
Write how the people are showing that they have listened to Jesus.

WE RESPOND

What are some things you can do to show Jesus that you have listened to him?

Fill in the circle beside the correct answer.

1. The _____ is the book of God's word.

   ○ Bible   ○ good news

2. The gospels are four of the books of the _____ that tell about Jesus' life and teaching.

   ○ New Testament   ○ Old Testament

3. We read about God's people who lived before Jesus in the _____ .

   ○ New Testament   ○ Old Testament

4. The word *gospel* means _____ .

   ○ good news   ○ Scripture

5. How do we show that we listen to God's word?

   _____

   _____

   _____

ASSESSMENT

Make a poster to show the two parts of the Bible. Explain each part.

We Respond in Faith ✝

Reflect & Pray

Holy Spirit, help me to listen to God's word.
Please help me share

_____

_____

_____

Key Words

Bible (p. 97)
Old Testament (p. 99)
New Testament (p. 101)
gospels (p. 101)

Remember

- The Bible is the book of God's word.
- The Old Testament is the first part of the Bible.
- The New Testament is the second part of the Bible.
- Jesus wants us to listen to his teachings.

OUR CATHOLIC LIFE

Catholic Newspapers

In the United States we have many Catholic newspapers. We can read about the ways people take care of the poor and make our community better. We can find explanations of Scripture stories that will be read at Mass and answers to questions about our faith.

Ask a family member to get a copy of the Catholic newspaper. Read about what is happening in the Catholic community.

SHARING FAITH
with My Family

Sharing What I Learned

Look at the pictures below. Use each picture to tell your family what you learned in this chapter.

For All to See

Your word is a lamp for my feet, a light for my path.

Psalm 119:105

Family Prayer

Together look through the family Bible. After you have located each section, pray together the words on the *For All to See* card.

• Find the beginning of the Old Testament.

• Find the last book of the Old Testament.

• Find the beginning of the New Testament.

• Find the beginning of each of the four gospels.

Bible Charades Have each family member act out his or her favorite Bible story. After someone guesses the story, let someone else take a turn.

Visit Sadlier's

www.WeBelieveweb.com

 Connect to the Catechism
For adult background and reflection, see paragraphs 104, 121, 124, and 127.

God Gives Us Laws

✝ We Gather in Prayer

Leader: Lord God, you give us life and love. Your laws help us to know how to love you and others. Show us how to follow you:

Reader 1: in our homes

Reader 2: in our parish

Reader 3: in our neighborhood

Reader 4: in our world.

All: The earth, LORD, is filled with your love; teach me your laws.

Psalm 119:64

Jesus taught us the Great Commandment.

WE GATHER

✝ *God, help us to know how to live as you want us to.*

What would you tell someone younger than you about crossing the street?

What would you tell a friend about wearing a bike helmet?

Why would you tell them these things?

WE BELIEVE

God the Father loves us very much. He cares about what happens to all of his children. God protects us by giving us laws to follow. God's laws are called **commandments**. When we follow God's laws, we will be happy.

 Matthew 22:35–39

One day Jesus was teaching. Someone asked him which commandment is the greatest. Jesus answered, "You shall love the Lord, your God, with all your heart, with all your soul, and with all your mind." Then he said, "You shall love your neighbor as yourself."

(Matthew 22:37, 39)

Jesus taught us ways to live the commandments. Jesus showed us how to love God, ourselves, and others. Jesus' teaching to love God and others is the **Great Commandment**. When we obey this commandment, we follow all of God's commandments.

Look at the pictures on these two pages. For each picture write how Jesus is living the Great Commandment.

_____

_____

WE RESPOND

What can you do to show that you love God and others as Jesus did?

Pray quietly. Ask Jesus to help you to love God. Ask him to help you to love others as you love yourself.

The Ten Commandments help us to live as God's children.

WE GATHER

✟ *God, we will do our best today to show our love for you and others.*

What is one rule that you follow at home?

What is one rule that you follow in school?

Do you think your parents and teachers also follow rules? Why?

WE BELIEVE

Many years before Jesus was born, God gave his people special laws. These laws are called the **Ten Commandments**. They are written in the Old Testament in the Bible.

When Jesus was growing up, he learned these commandments. All during his life, he obeyed these laws. He taught his followers to obey them, too.

We show our love for God and others by obeying the Ten Commandments. The commandments help us to live as God's children. The first three commandments help us to love God. The other seven commandments help us to love ourselves and others.

Key Word

Ten Commandments ten special laws God gave to his people

Here are the Ten Commandments. Remember that following them will lead you to love God and others.

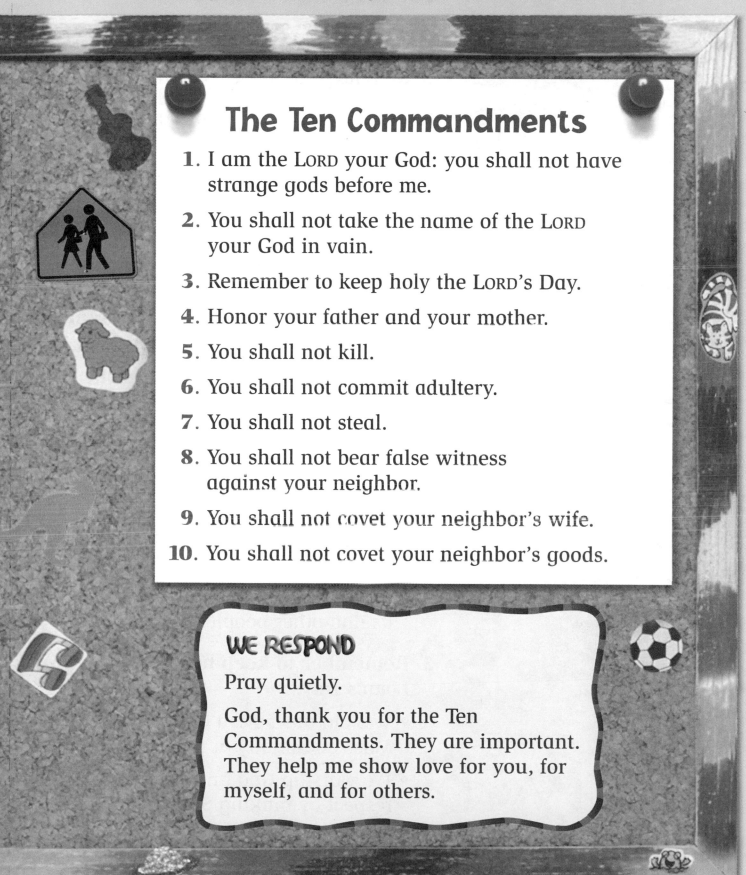

The Ten Commandments

1. I am the LORD your God: you shall not have strange gods before me.

2. You shall not take the name of the LORD your God in vain.

3. Remember to keep holy the LORD's Day.

4. Honor your father and your mother.

5. You shall not kill.

6. You shall not commit adultery.

7. You shall not steal.

8. You shall not bear false witness against your neighbor.

9. You shall not covet your neighbor's wife.

10. You shall not covet your neighbor's goods.

WE RESPOND

Pray quietly.

God, thank you for the Ten Commandments. They are important. They help me show love for you, for myself, and for others.

God wants us to show him our love and respect.

WE GATHER

✝ *God, help us to live as your children.*

How do you show love for your family and friends?

WE BELIEVE

God loves each of us very much. We must show God our love by following the first three commandments.

1. **I am the LORD your God: you shall not have strange gods before me.**

   - We believe that there is only one God.
   - We love and trust God more than anyone or anything.

2. **You shall not take the name of the LORD your God in vain.**

   - We speak God's name only with love and respect.
   - We praise God and ask him to bless us and other people.

3. **Remember to keep holy the LORD's Day.**

   - We join our parish each week for Mass on Sunday or Saturday evening.
   - We worship God and show him respect by making Sunday special.

Following these three commandments helps us to live as children of God.

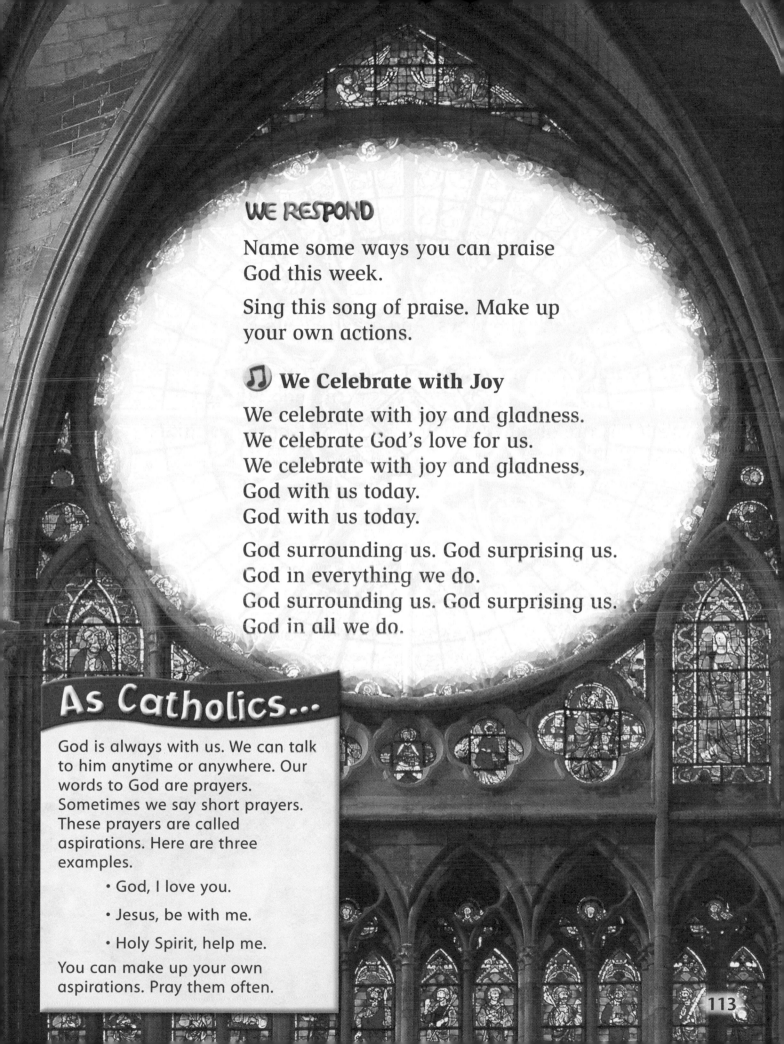

WE RESPOND

Name some ways you can praise God this week.

Sing this song of praise. Make up your own actions.

🎵 We Celebrate with Joy

We celebrate with joy and gladness.
We celebrate God's love for us.
We celebrate with joy and gladness,
God with us today.
God with us today.

God surrounding us. God surprising us.
God in everything we do.
God surrounding us. God surprising us.
God in all we do.

As Catholics...

God is always with us. We can talk to him anytime or anywhere. Our words to God are prayers. Sometimes we say short prayers. These prayers are called aspirations. Here are three examples.

- God, I love you.

- Jesus, be with me.

- Holy Spirit, help me.

You can make up your own aspirations. Pray them often.

God wants us to show that we love others as we love ourselves.

WE GATHER

✝ *Holy Spirit, help us.*

How do you and your family show respect for one another? How do you and your classmates show respect for one another?

Draw a ☺ next to the ways. Add others that show respect.

_____ We do not tease one another.　　_____ We help one another do good things.

_____ We take care of our things.　　_____ We share our things.

_____　　_____

_____　　_____

WE BELIEVE

God wants us to treat one another as brothers and sisters. In the fourth through the tenth commandments, we learn always to love ourselves and others.

Following the last seven commandments helps us to live as children of God.

Commandment	Ways to Follow the Commandment	
4 Honor your father and your mother.	• We obey our parents and all who care for us.	• We do not scream to get our way.
5 You shall not kill.	• We respect all human life.	• We do not fight or hurt anyone.
6 You shall not commit adultery.	• We respect our bodies and the bodies of others.	• We do not treat people like things. We protect everyone, especially those who cannot protect themselves.
7 You shall not steal.	• We take care of what we own. We are fair when playing. We share with those in need.	• We do not steal what other people own. We do not cheat.
8 You shall not bear false witness against your neighbor.	• We tell the truth.	• We do not say mean things about others.
9 You shall not covet your neighbor's wife.	• We show that we are happy and thankful for our family and friends.	• We do not get jealous of other people because of the friends they have.
10 You shall not covet your neighbor's goods.	• We show that we are happy and thankful for what we own.	• We do not get jealous of other people because of the things they own.

WE RESPOND

How can following the commandments help you to respect people?

Circle the correct answer. If you do not know the answer, circle ?

1. Jesus' teaching to love God and others is the Great Commandment.

   Yes   No   ?

2. We should always speak God's name with respect.

   Yes   No   ?

3. We can take things that we like from others.

   Yes   No   ?

4. Protecting the lives of everyone is one way we follow God's law.

   Yes   No   ?

5. Why are the Ten Commandments important?

   _____

   _____

Think of the Great Commandment. Write a story or draw a picture to show the ways you can love God and others.

We Respond in Faith

Reflect & Pray

Dear God, thank you for the gift of the Ten Commandments. I know that they are laws that

_____

_____

Key Words

commandments (p. 109)
Great Commandment (p. 109)
Ten Commandments (p. 110)

Remember

- Jesus taught us the Great Commandment.
- The Ten Commandments help us to live as God's children.
- God wants us to show him our love and respect.
- God wants us to show that we love others as we love ourselves.

OUR CATHOLIC LIFE

Living the Commandments

God wants us to follow the Ten Commandments even when we are playing games. We do this by following game rules, being honest, respecting other players, helping the team members who do not play as well as others, not saying mean words, and not doing mean things just to win a game.

SHARING FAITH
with My Family

Sharing What I Learned

Look at the pictures below. Use each picture to tell your family what you learned in this chapter.

For All to See

"The earth, LORD, is filled with your love; teach me your laws."
(Psalm 119:64)

Family Respect

Together make a large sign to put near the *For All to See* card. Print the word *respect* on a large sheet of paper. During the coming week, talk about specific ways your family can show respect for God, yourselves, and your neighbor. Write these ways on the sign.

Family Prayer Pledge

Pray together:

We shall love you, God, with our whole selves. We shall love our neighbors as ourselves.

 Connect to the Catechism
For adult background and reflection, see paragraphs 2055, 2059, 2067, and 2069.

✝ We Gather in Prayer

Leader: Let us celebrate the gift of God's laws. God gives us laws because he loves us and wants us to be happy. Listen to these words.

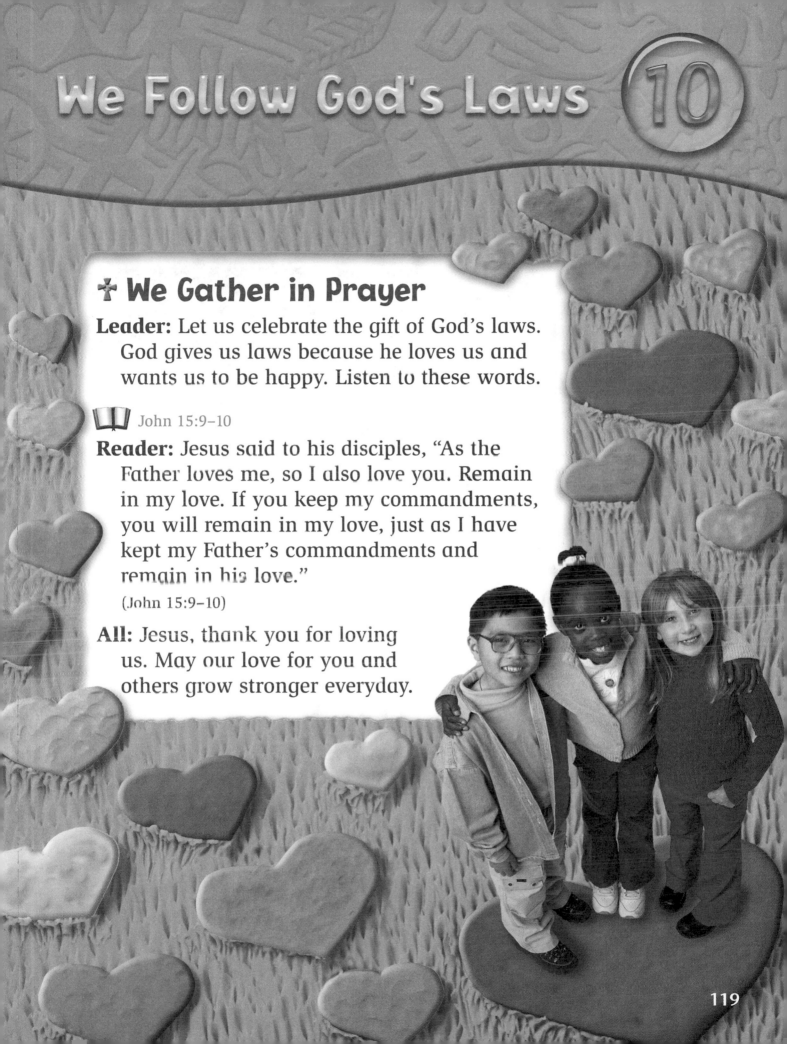 John 15:9–10

Reader: Jesus said to his disciples, "As the Father loves me, so I also love you. Remain in my love. If you keep my commandments, you will remain in my love, just as I have kept my Father's commandments and remain in his love."

(John 15:9–10)

All: Jesus, thank you for loving us. May our love for you and others grow stronger everyday.

Jesus wants us to follow the commandments.

WE GATHER

✝ *Jesus, help us to follow your example.*

There are choices that you make each day.
Think about one choice that you made today.

WE BELIEVE

Jesus made choices all during his life on earth.
He chose to love everyone. Jesus chose to help
people even when he felt tired. He chose to spend
time with people, both the poor and the rich.
Jesus made these choices even when others did
not agree with him.

Jesus wants us to follow his example of caring for everyone. He wants us to follow the commandments. Jesus knows that it is not always easy for us to choose to love God and others. That is why he sent the Holy Spirit to help us.

WE RESPOND

Jesus chose to love everyone. He reached out to feed hungry people. He welcomed children when they ran up to meet him.

How can you follow Jesus' example?

Ask the Holy Spirit to guide you in making choices.

With a partner, make up a tune or a special beat for this prayer.

Holy Spirit, help me to speak
Kind words to others all this week.

Holy Spirit, help me to share,
To do kind acts, and to be fair.

Holy Spirit, help me to see,
Jesus in everyone around me.

Now add your own verse.
Write the words here.

_____

_____

God gives each person free will.

WE GATHER

✝ *Holy Spirit, fill our hearts with love.*

What are the differences between robots and people?

 Write **P** by the sentences about people.
Write **R** by the sentences about robots.

They have feelings and can love others. _____

They can choose between right and wrong. _____

They cannot think. _____

They cannot make their own decisions. _____

WE BELIEVE

God never forces us to love and obey him. God lets us choose to love him and others. He lets us choose between following the commandments and not following them. God's gift to us that allows us to make choices is **free will**.

When we freely choose to do something, we are responsible for what we do. We are responsible for what happens because of our choices. Here are two choices Erica might make.

Key Word

free will God's gift to us that allows us to make choices

122

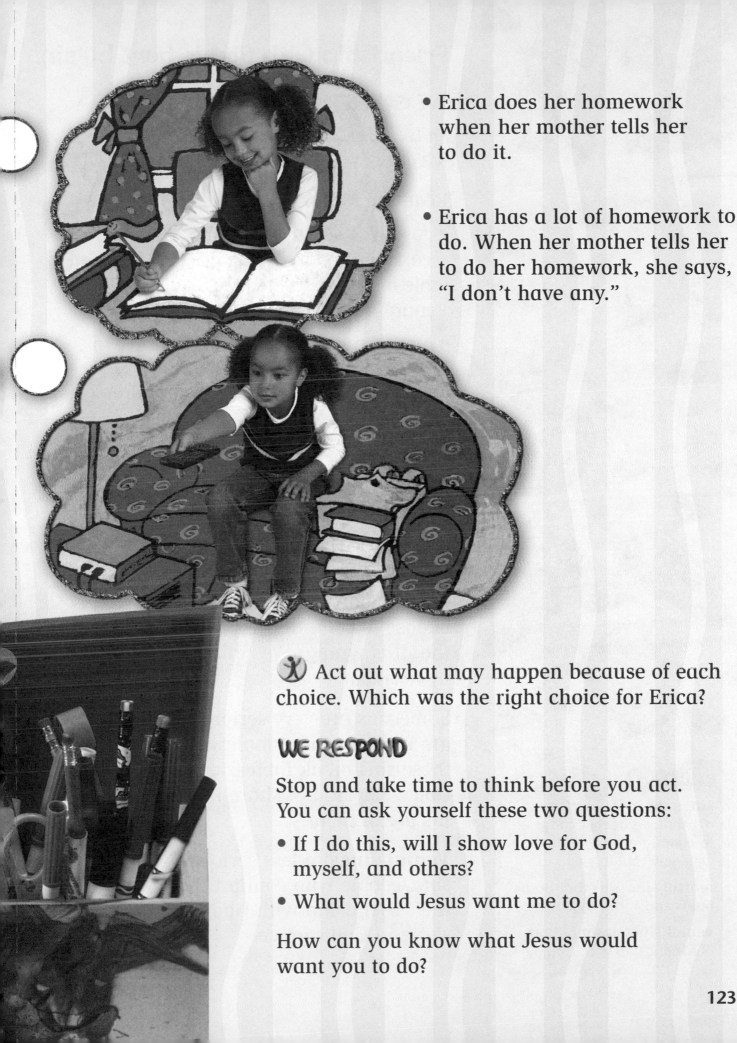

• Erica does her homework when her mother tells her to do it.

• Erica has a lot of homework to do. When her mother tells her to do her homework, she says, "I don't have any."

Act out what may happen because of each choice. Which was the right choice for Erica?

WE RESPOND

Stop and take time to think before you act. You can ask yourself these two questions:

• If I do this, will I show love for God, myself, and others?

• What would Jesus want me to do?

How can you know what Jesus would want you to do?

Friendship with God is hurt by sin.

WE GATHER

✝ *Holy Spirit, help us to think before we act.*

Read the following stories.

- José was setting the table. He was carrying too many dishes. He dropped his mom's favorite mug, and the mug broke.

- Nora's mom would not let her go to her friend's house. So Nora threw her mom's favorite mug on the floor. The mug broke into little pieces.

How are these stories the same? How are these stories different?

WE BELIEVE

Commit is another word for "do." **Sin** is any thought, word, or act that we freely choose to commit even though we know that it is wrong. We cannot commit sin by accident.

Some sins are very serious. These sins are **mortal sins**. People who commit these sins break their friendship with God. They do not share in God's grace, his life in them.

Venial sins are less serious than mortal sins. People who commit these sins hurt their friendship with God. But they still share in God's grace.

Key Words

sin a thought, word, or act that we freely choose to commit even though we know that it is wrong

mortal sins sins that break our friendship with God

venial sins sins that hurt our friendship with God

When we commit sin, we hurt ourselves and others, too. But it is important to always remember:

- God never stops loving us.
- God will always forgive us when we are sorry.

WE RESPOND

How can you show God that his friendship is important to you?

 Write to God about what you have learned today.

_____

_____

_____

_____

As Catholics...

A person who chose to follow God's laws was Saint Philip Neri. Philip was a priest in Rome. He helped the sick and the poor. Philip told many people that Jesus loved and cared for them. He helped people understand that God would always forgive them.

We know that Jesus loves and cares for each one of us, too.

Jesus taught us about God's forgiveness.

WE GATHER

✞ *God, thank you for your love and friendship.*

How do you feel when you forgive someone?
How do you feel when someone forgives you?

WE BELIEVE

Jesus told stories to teach about God's love and forgiveness. He taught that God always loves us and is ready to forgive us. Another word for God's love and forgiveness is **mercy**.

This play comes from a story Jesus told to teach about God's mercy.

📖 Luke 15:11–24

All: There was a loving father who had two sons. One day the younger son asked his father for his share of the family's money.

Son: Father, I need money.
Goodbye. I've got to run.
I am going away.
I just want to have fun.

All: The young man did not always follow the Ten Commandments. He spent his money on parties and new friends.

Friends: You've lost all your money.
No more parties for you.
We don't really care
What happens to you.

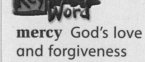
mercy God's love and forgiveness

All: The young man began to think about the choices he had made. He remembered his father's love.

Son: I am so sorry now.
Just look what I have done!
Can my father forgive me?
I'm a very selfish son!

All: The young man was on the road home when his father saw him. The father ran to welcome him back.

Father: Son, I really missed you
And I can hardly wait
To show my love for you.
Now let's all celebrate!

"Then the celebration began."
(Luke 15:24)

The father in this story showed mercy to his son. God the Father shows each of us his mercy. He will always forgive us when we are sorry.

Act out the story of the father and the son. Then talk about the choices the father and son made.

WE RESPOND

How do you feel knowing that God is always ready to forgive you? Thank God for his great mercy.

127

Review

Review

Review

Grade 2
Chapter 10

Use these words to complete sentences 1–4.

mortal	mercy	commit
commandments	free will	venial

1. Sins that hurt out friendship with God are

____________________ sins.

2. Sins that break our friendship with God are

____________________ sins.

3. Jesus wants us to follow the ____________________.

4. Another word for God's love and forgiveness

is ____________________ .

5. What is the gift of free will?

____

____

ASSESSMENT

Jesus told a story about a father who showed mercy to his son. Use your own words to tell this story. Draw a picture for each part of the story.

We Respond in Faith

Reflect & Pray

Holy Spirit, when I have to choose between doing the right thing and the wrong thing,

_____

_____

Key Words

free will (p. 122)

sin (p. 124)

mortal sins (p. 124)

venial sins (p. 124)

mercy (p. 126)

Remember

- Jesus wants us to follow the commandments.
- God gives each person free will.
- Friendship with God is hurt by sin.
- Jesus taught us about God's forgiveness.

OUR CATHOLIC LIFE

Choosing Friends

One important decision we make in life is choosing our friends. Good friends want the best for one another.

When you choose a person to be your friend, you may want to think about these questions.

- How do I act when I am with this person?
- What kind of choices do I make when I am with this person?
- Does this person want the best for me?

SHARING FAITH
with My Family

Sharing What I Learned

Look at the pictures below. Use each picture to tell your family what you learned in this chapter.

For All to See

"If you choose you can keep the commandments; it is loyalty to do his will."
(Sirach 15:15)

What's Your Choice?

Think about and discuss these choices.

• You have just won two hundred dollars. Will you keep all the money or will you share it?

• Everybody in your family is home tonight. Will you join the family in doing something together?

Family Scripture Meditation

Share the story of the father and his son (Luke 15:11–24). Put yourselves in the father or son's place. Then talk about the choices you made. Pray together, "God, thank you for your love and forgiveness."

Visit Sadlier's
www.WEBELIEVEweb.com

 Connect to the Catechism
For adult background and reflection, see paragraphs 2074, 1730, 1850, and 981.

130

We Prepare for the Sacrament of Forgiveness

✝ **We Gather in Prayer**

Leader: Jesus is our Good Shepherd.

All: Jesus, we are the sheep of your flock.

Leader: Jesus, may we never wander far from you.

All: Jesus, Good Shepherd, hear us.

Leader: Jesus, when we have not followed your ways,

All: Forgive us and lead us back to your loving ways.

Jesus invites us to celebrate God's forgiveness.

WE GATHER

✝ *Jesus, lead us in your loving ways.*

Why do you think friends and family members forgive each other?

How do they show their forgiveness?

WE BELIEVE

When Jesus was on earth, he forgave people's sins. He showed them God's mercy. He wanted people to know that God would always love and forgive them. Jesus wanted them to understand God's forgiveness. So he told the story of the lost sheep.

 Luke 15:4–6

There was a shepherd who took care of one hundred sheep. One day one of the sheep wandered away. The shepherd left the other ninety-nine sheep. He searched for the lost one until he found it. The shepherd put the sheep on his shoulders and carried it. When he got home, he called together his friends. He said, "Rejoice with me because I have found my lost sheep." (Luke 15:6)

Sin separates us from God and one another. When we sin, we are like the lost sheep. But Jesus has given us a way to come back together again. The word *reconciliation* comes from a word that means "coming back together again."

Jesus has given us a way to receive God's forgiveness. The Church celebrates this forgiveness in the sacrament of Penance and Reconciliation.

WE RESPOND

Think about Jesus' story of the lost sheep. How does it help you to know more about God's love?

Pray together.

Jesus, thank you for giving us a way to celebrate God's forgiveness and love.

133

Jesus shares God's forgiveness and peace in the sacrament of Penance and Reconciliation.

WE GATHER

✝ *Jesus, our Good Shepherd, take care of each one of us.*

🏃 Number these sentences in order to make a reconciliation story.

_____ Teresa did not feel right because she had lied.

_____ Teresa's mom hugged her and said, "I forgive you."

_____ Teresa said, "I'm sorry, Mom. I lied to you. I won't do it again."

_____ Teresa told her mom a lie.

WE BELIEVE

God's love and forgiveness give us peace. When we sin, we are not at peace with God, ourselves, or others.

In the gospels we read some stories about people who were not at peace with God. Jesus offered them God's love. He forgave their sins. Jesus shared God's mercy and peace with them.

Jesus gives us a way to find peace, too. He shares God's forgiveness and peace with us. In the sacrament of **Penance and Reconciliation** we receive and celebrate God's forgiveness of our sins. We can call this sacrament the sacrament of Reconciliation.

Jesus gave his apostles the power to forgive sin in his name. Today in the sacrament of Reconciliation, bishops and priests forgive sins in Jesus' name. They received this power to forgive sins in the sacrament of Holy Orders.

WE RESPOND

Why does the sacrament of Reconciliation bring us God's peace?

Penance and Reconciliation
the sacrament in which we receive and celebrate God's forgiveness of our sins

Pray quietly. Ask Jesus to help you to be at peace with God, yourself, and others.

We examine our conscience.

WE GATHER

✝ *Holy Spirit, send us your peace.*

It is important to stop and think about things that we do.

Think about the things that you did yesterday. Talk about some of them.

WE BELIEVE

God has given each person a **conscience**. This gift helps a person to know what is right and what is wrong.

We can prepare to celebrate the sacrament of Reconciliation by examining our conscience. This means we think about our thoughts, words, and actions.

The Holy Spirit helps us to remember the choices we have made. We think about whether or not we have followed God's laws. We think about the ways we have or have not followed the Ten Commandments.

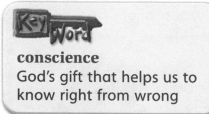

conscience
God's gift that helps us to know right from wrong

As Catholics...

Many Catholics make an examination of conscience during their nighttime prayer. They think about ways they have or have not followed Jesus' example that day. They ask themselves how they have respected God, themselves, and others. They then ask the Holy Spirit to help them make good choices. Ask the Holy Spirit to help you to make good choices, too.

WE RESPOND

When you examine your conscience, you can ask yourself questions like these. As you read these questions, talk to God quietly about your answers.

Respect for God

• Did I always speak God's name in the right way?

• Did I pray to God?

Respect for Myself

• Did I take care of my body?

• Was I grateful for all the gifts God has given to me?

Respect for Family and Others

• Did I obey my parents and all those who care for me?

• Did I hurt someone by what I said or did?

Think about other questions you can ask yourself to examine your conscience.

Write one of them.

_____

_____

_____

We tell God we are sorry for our sins.

WE GATHER

✝ *God, please give us your mercy and peace.*

What would you say to make up with someone you hurt?

How could you show this person that you really are sorry?

WE BELIEVE

Another word for sorrow is *contrition*. We tell God we are sorry for our sins in the sacrament of Reconciliation. We also tell God we will try not to sin again. We do both of these things when we say a special prayer of sorrow. We call this prayer an act of contrition.

Here is an act of contrition that many people pray. Prepare for the sacrament of Reconciliation by learning it.

Act of Contrition

My God,
I am sorry for my sins with all my heart.
In choosing to do wrong
and failing to do good,
I have sinned against you
whom I should love above all things.
I firmly intend, with your help,
to do penance,
to sin no more,
and to avoid whatever leads me to sin.
Our Savior Jesus Christ
suffered and died for us.
In his name, my God, have mercy.

Use a different colored crayon to underline each of the following words of the prayer:

- words that tell God we are sorry

- words that promise to try not to sin again

- words that ask God to forgive us in Jesus' name.

WE RESPOND

How can you show God you are truly sorry?

Pray together the Act of Contrition on this page.

Fill in the circle next to the correct answer.

1. Our _____ helps us to know right from wrong.

   ○ conscience   ○ contrition

2. We are not at peace with God, ourselves, and others when we _____.

   ○ sin   ○ love

3. Reconciliation is a sacrament of _____.

   ○ forgiveness   ○ forgetting

4. The _____ is a prayer of sorrow.

   ○ Sign of the Cross   ○ Act of Contrition

5. Write two ways that you can prepare for the sacrament of Reconciliation.

   _____

   _____

   _____

Jesus' story about the lost sheep on page 132 is about reconciliation with God. Draw a picture to tell the story.

We Respond in Faith

Reflect & Pray

Write your own prayer to tell God you are sorry for your sins.

_____

_____

Key Words

Penance and Reconciliation (p. 135)

conscience (p. 136)

Remember

- Jesus invites us to celebrate God's forgiveness.
- Jesus shares God's forgiveness and peace in the sacrament of Penance and Reconciliation.
- We examine our conscience.
- We tell God we are sorry for our sins.

OUR CATHOLIC LIFE

When Do We Celebrate?

All of us are in need of God's forgiveness. The Church encourages us to celebrate the sacrament of Reconciliation. If we sin in a way that breaks our friendship with God, we must tell these mortal sins to the priest. We should also tell the venial sins that hurt our friendship with God and with one another. In the sacrament of Reconciliation we receive forgiveness and are at peace with God and with one another.

SHARING FAITH
with My Family

Sharing What I Learned

Look at the pictures below. Use each picture to tell your family what you learned in this chapter.

For All to See and Pray

Act of Contrition

My God,
I am sorry for my sins with all my heart.
In choosing to do wrong
and failing to do good,
I have sinned against you
whom I should love above all things.
I firmly intend, with your help,
to do penance,
to sin no more,
and to avoid whatever leads me to sin.
Our Savior Jesus Christ
suffered and died for us.
In his name, my God, have mercy.

Connect to the Catechism
For adult background and reflection,
see paragraphs 1441, 1446, 1451, and 1454.

✝ We Gather in Prayer

♪ We Come to Ask Forgiveness

We come to ask your forgiveness, O Lord,
and we seek forgiveness from each other.
Sometimes we build up walls instead
   of bridges to peace,
and we ask your forgiveness,
   O Lord.

For the times when we've been
   rude and selfish,
for the times when we have
   been unkind;
and for the times we refused
   to help our friends in need,
we ask your forgiveness,
   O Lord.

We ask for God's forgiveness in the sacrament of Reconciliation.

WE GATHER

✝ *God, we want to celebrate your forgiveness.*

Think about TV shows or movies you have watched in the past few weeks. Tell about those that were stories of forgiveness.

WE BELIEVE

There are times in our lives that we all need to ask for forgiveness. We ask God for forgiveness in the sacrament of Reconciliation.

When we celebrate the sacrament of Reconciliation, we think about the ways we have shown or not shown love for God and for others. This is an examination of conscience. We are sorry for our sins and promise not to sin again. This is **contrition**.

We tell our sins to the priest. This is called **confession**.

The priest tells us to say a prayer or to do a kind act to make up for our sins. This is called **a penance**.

Key Words

contrition being sorry for our sins and promising not to sin again

confession telling our sins to the priest in the sacrament of Reconciliation

a penance a prayer or a kind act we do to make up for our sins

absolution God's forgiveness of our sins by the priest in the sacrament of Reconciliation

We say an act of contrition to tell God we are sorry. We promise not to sin again. The priest acting in the name of Jesus forgives our sins. This is called **absolution**. The word *absolution* comes from a word that means "washing away."

These steps are always part of the sacrament of Reconciliation. When we celebrate the sacrament of Reconciliation, we meet with the priest. He acts in the name of Jesus. We may sit and face the priest or kneel behind a screen.

WE RESPOND

When you celebrate Reconciliation, you will receive a penance. Sometimes the priest will tell you to say a prayer. Sometimes he will tell you to do a kind act.

What are you telling God when you do the penance the priest gives you?

We celebrate God's forgiveness in the sacrament of Reconciliation.

WE GATHER

 God, we trust in your love and forgiveness.

This picture shows Lucy getting ready to celebrate the sacrament of Reconciliation. She is examining her conscience.

 Write a question she can ask herself.

_____

_____

WE BELIEVE

This is what happened when Lucy went to Father Rob to celebrate the sacrament of Reconciliation.

- Father Rob welcomed Lucy, and they both made the sign of the cross.

- Lucy listened as Father Rob read a story from the Bible. The story was about God's forgiveness.

- Lucy confessed her sins to Father Rob.

- Father Rob and Lucy talked about what she could do to make right choices. Then Father gave Lucy a penance. Lucy will do her penance after the celebration of the sacrament.

- Lucy prayed an act of contrition.
- Lucy received absolution, or forgiveness, from her sins. Father Rob stretched out his right hand over Lucy's head. He said the following words to Lucy.

"God, the Father of mercies,
through the death and resurrection
    of his Son
has reconciled the world to himself
and sent the Holy Spirit among us
for the forgiveness of sins;
through the ministry of the Church
may God give you pardon and peace,
and I absolve you from your sins
in the name of the Father,
    and of the Son, †
and of the Holy Spirit."
Lucy answered, "Amen."

- Then Father Rob and Lucy praised and thanked God for his love and forgiveness. Father told Lucy, "Go in peace."

As Catholics...

The parish priest is always willing to help us. He listens to us and helps us to follow Jesus. We tell the priest our sins in the sacrament of Reconciliation. The priest cannot tell anyone the sins we confess.

Who are the priests who will celebrate Reconciliation with you?

We can celebrate the sacrament of Reconciliation as Lucy did. God is always willing to give us his mercy and peace when we are sorry.

WE RESPOND

How do you think celebrating the sacrament of Reconciliation will help you?

We celebrate the sacrament of Reconciliation with our parish community.

WE GATHER

✝ *God, we celebrate your forgiveness.*

You gather with your parish community at Mass on Sunday. When are other times your parish community gathers?

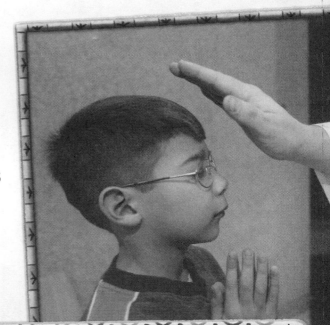

WE BELIEVE

Our parish community sometimes gathers to celebrate the sacrament of Reconciliation together. This helps us to see that all of us need forgiveness.

This is what happens during that celebration.

- The parish community sings a song. Then we are welcomed by the priest.

- We listen to readings from the Bible. These readings are about God's love and forgiveness.

- The priest talks to us about the readings.

- We listen to questions that are part of an examination of conscience.

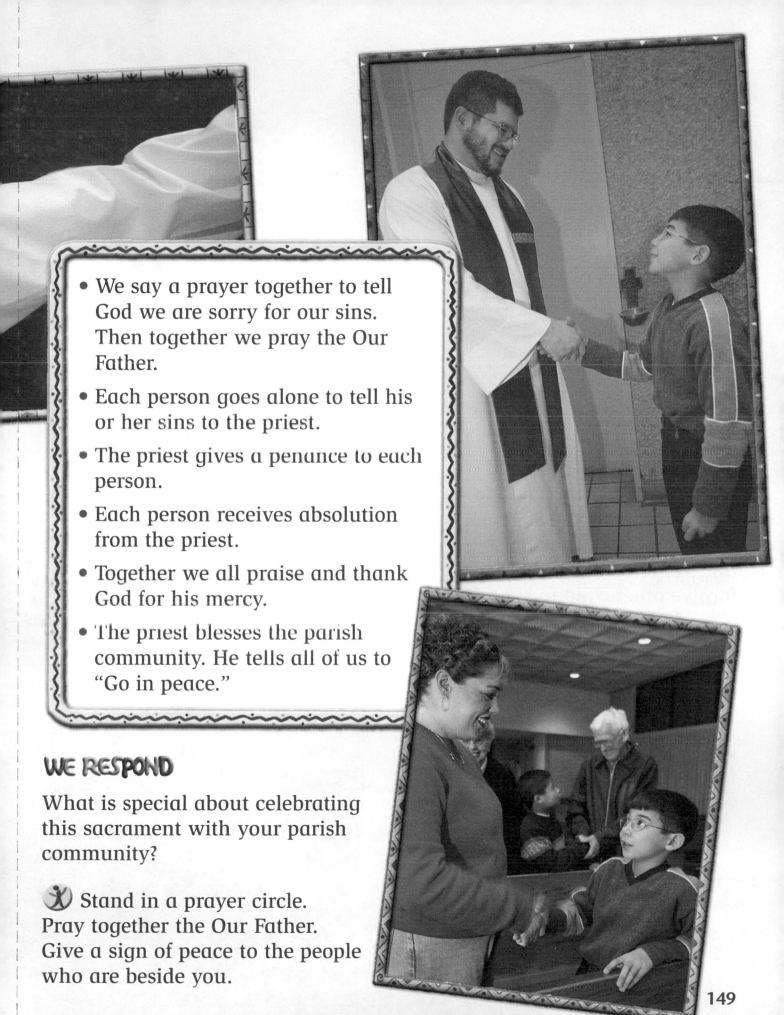

- We say a prayer together to tell God we are sorry for our sins. Then together we pray the Our Father.

- Each person goes alone to tell his or her sins to the priest.

- The priest gives a penance to each person.

- Each person receives absolution from the priest.

- Together we all praise and thank God for his mercy.

- The priest blesses the parish community. He tells all of us to "Go in peace."

WE RESPOND

What is special about celebrating this sacrament with your parish community?

Stand in a prayer circle. Pray together the Our Father. Give a sign of peace to the people who are beside you.

Jesus wants us to forgive others.

WE GATHER

✝ *Jesus, thank you for your gift of peace.*

Do you ever ask others to forgive you? Why? What do you say to someone when they ask you to forgive them?

WE BELIEVE

 Matthew 18:21–23

One day Peter asked Jesus, "Lord, if my brother sins against me, how often must I forgive him? As many as seven times?" Jesus answered, "I say to you, not seven times but seventy-seven times." (Matthew 18:21, 22)

In this story, Jesus is telling us that we should always forgive others. When we celebrate the sacrament of Reconciliation, we receive God's forgiveness and peace. Jesus wants us to forgive others and to share God's gift of peace with them.

Jesus wants us to be peacemakers

- wherever we are
- whenever we can
- in whatever we do.

WE RESPOND

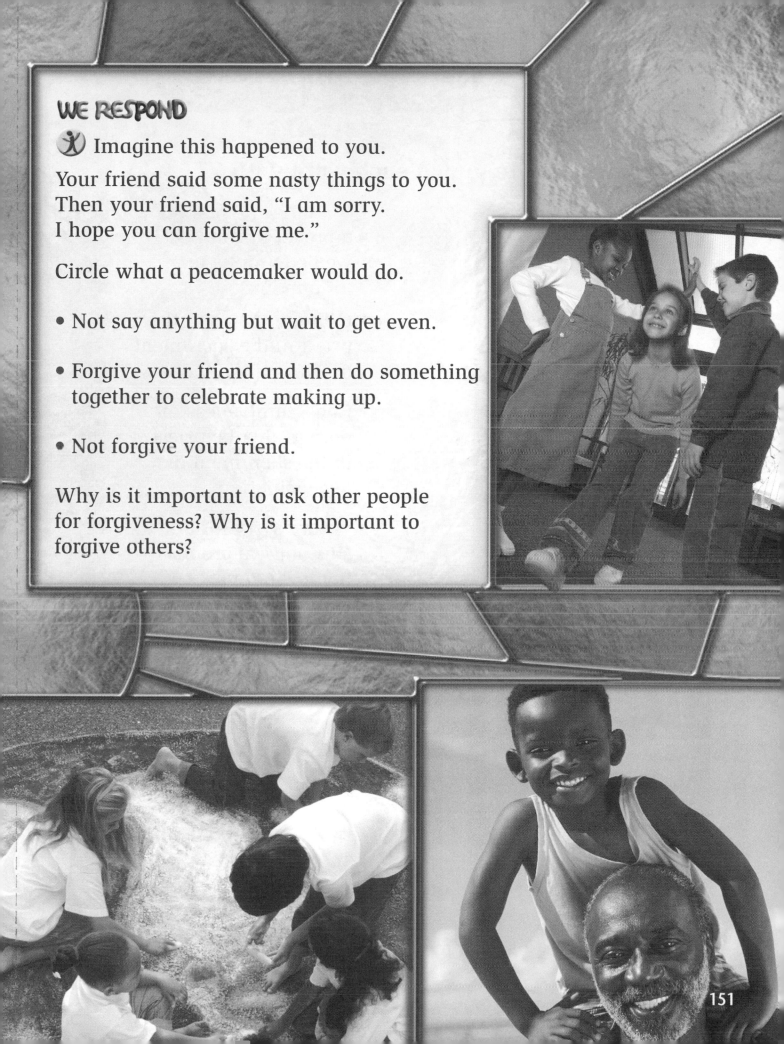 Imagine this happened to you.

Your friend said some nasty things to you. Then your friend said, "I am sorry. I hope you can forgive me."

Circle what a peacemaker would do.

- Not say anything but wait to get even.

- Forgive your friend and then do something together to celebrate making up.

- Not forgive your friend.

Why is it important to ask other people for forgiveness? Why is it important to forgive others?

Review

Draw a line to match each word with its definition.

1. absolution •

2. a penance •

3. confession •

4. contrition •

• a prayer or kind act we do to make up for our sins

• telling our sins to the priest in the sacrament of Reconciliation

• God's forgiveness of our sins by the priest in the sacrament of Reconciliation

• we are sorry for our sins and we promise not to sin again

Use your own words to complete the sentence.

5. Jesus told us about forgiving others. He said that

_____.

ASSESSMENT

Think about Lucy's celebration of the sacrament of Reconciliation. Put the following words in order to tell about her celebration.

act of contrition, examination of conscience, absolution, confession, Bible reading

We Respond in Faith

Reflect & Pray

Draw a picture or write about what it means to "Go in peace."

Key Words

contrition (p. 145)
confession (p. 145)
a penance (p. 145)
absolution (p. 145)

Remember

- We ask for God's forgiveness in the sacrament of Reconciliation.
- We celebrate God's forgiveness in the sacrament of Reconciliation.
- We celebrate the sacrament of Reconciliation with our parish community.
- Jesus wants us to forgive others.

OUR CATHOLIC LIFE

A Peacemaker

Saint Francis of Assisi is known as a peacemaker. When one town went to war against another, Francis asked them to put away their weapons. He helped them come to a peaceful agreement. Francis wrote a prayer for peace that we still pray today. He wrote, "Lord, make me an instrument of your peace."

SHARING FAITH
with My Family

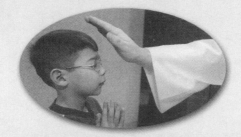

Sharing What I Learned

Look at the pictures below. Use each picture to tell your family what you learned in this chapter.

For All to See

Jesus said, "Peace be with you."
(John 20:21)

Family Examination of Conscience

Each night this week, share these questions for an examination of conscience. Allow a brief time of silence after each question is read. Add questions of your own. Then pray the Our Father.

• Did I make God an important part of my day? How?

• Did I appreciate the many gifts God has given me?

• Was I respectful?

• Did I share with others?

• Did I help other people?

• Did I forgive those who hurt me?

• Did I ask for forgiveness from someone I hurt?

• _____

Visit Sadlier's
www.WeBelieveweb.com

Connect to the Catechism
For adult background and reflection, see paragraphs 1425, 1455, 1468, and 1469.

"In his love Christ has filled us with joy as we prepare to celebrate his birth."

Advent II Preface, Eucharistic Prayer

Advent is a season of waiting and preparing.

WE GATHER

🎵 **Stay Awake**

Stay awake, be ready.
You do not know the hour when the
Lord is coming.
Stay awake, be ready.
The Lord is coming soon!
Alleluia, alleluia!
The Lord is coming soon!

WE BELIEVE

The season of Advent is a time to prepare to celebrate the coming of Jesus. During Advent we watch and wait.

We watch for signs of God's love in the world. We can see signs of God's love in:

- the gifts of his creation
- the loving ways people treat one another
- the work of the Church.

Think about some other signs of God's love. Talk about them.

Jesus is the greatest sign of God's love. Jesus is the Son of God who came into the world. Jesus brings life and light to all people.

The four weeks of Advent are filled with joy and hope. We celebrate this season at home and in our parish. One way of celebrating is by gathering around an Advent wreath. This wreath is made of evergreen branches and has four candles. There is one candle for each week of Advent.

Week One

 On the first Sunday of Advent we light the first purple candle.

 On the second Sunday of Advent we light the first and second purple candles.

Week Two

 On the third Sunday of Advent we light the first and second purple candles and the rose candle.

 On the fourth Sunday of Advent we light all four candles.

Week Three

Show how the wreath changes as the weeks of Advent go by.

We light the Advent wreath to remind us to watch and wait for the coming of Jesus. The light from the candles reminds us that Jesus is the Light of the World.

Week Four

WE RESPOND

Jesus asks us to share his light with others. During the season of Advent, we can help people to see God's love.

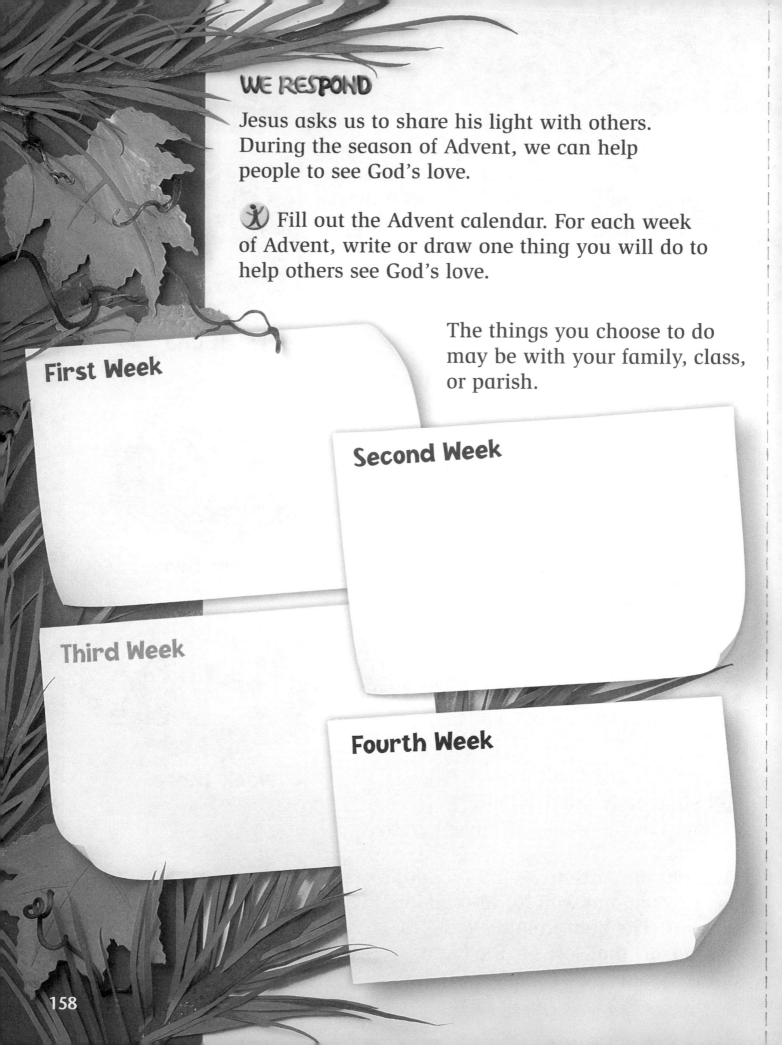 Fill out the Advent calendar. For each week of Advent, write or draw one thing you will do to help others see God's love.

The things you choose to do may be with your family, class, or parish.

First Week

Second Week

Third Week

Fourth Week

✝ We Respond in Prayer

Leader: Praised be the God of joy and hope.

All: Jesus, you are the Light of the World.

Leader: Let us listen to a reading from the Old Testament.

"The people who walked in darkness
have seen a great light." (Isaiah 9:1)

The word of the Lord.

All: Thanks be to God.

Leader: Let us pray. To our hearts and to our homes,

All: Come, Lord Jesus!

Leader: To our families and friends,

All: Come, Lord Jesus!

Leader: To people everywhere,

All: Come, Lord Jesus!

Leader: Let us walk in the light of Jesus!

All: Come, Lord Jesus!

SHARING FAITH
with My Family

Sharing What I Learned

Look at the pictures below. Use each picture to tell your family what you learned in this chapter.

Around the Table

With your family, make special place mats for Sunday meals during Advent. Decorate large pieces of paper or fabric with gifts of creation, which are signs of God's love. Write Advent messages and prayers on the place mat, too. Use these messages and add your own!

Come, Lord Jesus!
Jesus is the Light of the World.
We wait for Jesus with hope and joy.

An Advent Prayer

At your family meals, place a candle in the center of the table. Ask an adult to light it. Then pray together.

Jesus, you are the Light of the World.
As we prepare to receive you into our hearts this Christmas,
help us to share your light with one another,
with everyone we meet,
and with the whole world.
Amen.

Visit Sadlier's
www.WeBelieveweb.com

Connect to the Catechism
For adult background and reflection, see paragraph 524.

Christmas

14

Advent | **Christmas** | Ordinary Time | Lent | Three Days | Easter | Ordinary Time

"Glory to God in the highest."

Luke 2:14

Christmas is a season to give glory to God.

WE GATHER

Who are the people you celebrate Christmas with? Who do you think about when you celebrate?

WE BELIEVE

During the Christmas season, we celebrate something wonderful. We celebrate God's greatest gift to us, his Son, Jesus. We give glory to God for the birth of Jesus.

 Act out this Christmas play.

 Luke 2:1–20

Narrator: During that time before Jesus' birth, a new rule was made. All men had to go back to the town of their father's family. They had to sign a list and be counted.

Joseph was from Bethlehem, the city of David. So Joseph had to go to Bethlehem with Mary.

"While they were there, the time came for her to have her child, and she gave birth to her firstborn son. She wrapped him in swaddling clothes and laid him in a manger, because there was no room for them in the inn." (Luke 2:6–7)

On the hills nearby, some shepherds were watching their sheep.

Shepherds: Look! Look! The sky is filled with light!

Narrator: All of a sudden, an angel appeared. The shepherds were afraid.

Angel: "Do not be afraid; for behold, I proclaim to you good news of great joy that will be for all the people. For today in the city of David a savior has been born for you who is Messiah and Lord. You will find an infant wrapped in swaddling clothes and lying in a manger." (Luke 2:10–12)

Narrator: Suddenly, many angels were there. They were all praising God and saying:

All Angels: "Glory to God in the highest." (Luke 2:14)

Narrator: The shepherds hurried to Bethlehem. They found Mary and Joseph, and the baby lying in the manger. The shepherds told them what the angels had said about this child. All were amazed. The shepherds went back to their fields, saying:

Shepherds: Praise God! Glory and praise to God forever! Amen!

The Christmas season lasts about two weeks. It begins on Christmas Day, December 25. The special color of the Christmas season is white. White is a color of light and joy. You will see this color during the celebration of the Mass.

During the Christmas season, we celebrate that Jesus is the Light of the World. He is with us now and forever.

We remember this all during the season, especially when we take part in Mass.

WE RESPOND

Decorate this banner.
Who will you share this good news with?
How will you share it?

Jesus is with us Now and Forever

✝ We Respond in Prayer

Leader: Blessed be the name of the Lord.

All: Now and for ever.

Leader: Lord our God,
   we praise you for the light of creation:
   the sun, the moon, and the stars of
      the night.

   We praise you for Jesus Christ, your Son:
   he is Emmanuel, God-with-us,
      the Prince of Peace,
   who fills us with the wonder of
      your love.

All: We praise you, Lord God.

🎵 O Come, All Ye Faithful

O come, all ye faithful,
joyful and triumphant,
O come ye, O come ye to Bethlehem;
Come and behold him,
born the King of angels;

O come, let us adore him,
O come, let us adore him,
O come, let us adore him,
Christ, the Lord!

CHRISTMAS

SHARING FAITH
with My Family

Sharing What I Learned

Look at the pictures below. Use each picture to tell your family what you learned in this chapter.

For All to See and Pray

The Christmas season is a good time to bless your home. Together with your family, pray this blessing.

Lord, creator of heaven and earth,
    bless our home.
Make it a place of peace and love.
May all who live here bring
    the light and love of Christ
    to one another.
May we welcome visitors with joy.
May we always care for the weak
    and the poor.
We ask this through Christ
    our Lord.

Amen.

Visit Sadlier's

www.WeBelieveweb.com

Connect to the Catechism
For adult background and reflection, see paragraph 526.

Assessment

**Grade 2
Unit 2**

Circle the letter beside the correct answer.

1. God will _____ forgive us if we are sorry.

   a. sometimes   **b.** never   **c.** always

2. _____ is God's forgiveness of our sins by the priest in the sacrament of Reconciliation.

   a. Absolution   **b.** Celebration   **c.** Contrition

3. God's gift that allows us to make choices is _____.

   a. penance   **b.** free will   **c.** mercy

4. The _____ Testament is the part of the Bible about Jesus and the beginning of the Church.

   a. New   **b.** Old   **c.** Free

Draw a line to match the sentence parts.

5. An act of contrition   •   • helps us to know right from wrong.

6. The Great Commandment •   • is a prayer of sorrow.

7. God's gift of conscience •   • is Jesus' teaching to love God and others.

8–10. Tell three things you have learned about the Ten Commandments.

Look at the two pictures. Write two different things that each child can choose to do.

The child could choose to

_____

_____

_____

_____.

The child could choose to

_____

_____

_____

_____.

Circle the choice Jesus would want each child to make.

Choose one of these projects. Do your work on a separate piece of paper.

• Use your own words to write an act of contrition.

• Make a poster to show what you have learned about the Bible.

Jesus Gives Himself in the Eucharist

UNIT 3 SHARING FAITH as a Family

Five Ways to Help Your Child Pay Attention During Mass

Sunday morning can be a test of patience for parents when children whine about going to church. Catholic liturgy can be adult-focused, and often a child is being honest when he or she complains about not understanding it. Here are five ideas for dealing with this situation.

1. Read the gospel together beforehand. Stories about Jesus interest children, and they tend to be attentive when the story is familiar.

2. Teach your child the responses. This helps him or her to take part in the back-and-forth exchange between presider and assembly.

3. Point out what the presider is doing. Help your child focus on one particular gesture during each

Mass. For example, when does the priest make the sign of the cross, lift his hands, or bow?

4. Encourage your child to look for certain symbols during Mass. This could be the chalice, the lectionary, the color of the priest's vestments, or a candle.

5. Ask your child after Mass to name one thing he or she heard during the homily. If done without pressure, this can be a fun-filled learning experience.

This piece-by-piece approach may not end a child's restlessness during Mass. It can, however, help increase understanding and awareness over a period of time.

From the Catechism

"Parents have the mission of teaching their children to pray and to discover their vocation as children of God."

(Catechism of the Catholic Church, 2226)

What Your Child Will Learn in Unit 3

Unit 3 is all about the Eucharist, presented in ways that second graders can grasp and appreciate. The children will understand that Jesus gave us the gift of himself at the Last Supper. At Mass, we remember what Jesus did at the Last Supper. Thus, the children will perceive the Mass as both a sacrifice and a meal. The rest of the unit details each part of the Mass (the Introductory Rites, the Liturgy of the Word, the Liturgy of the Eucharist, and the Concluding Rite). The various roles of all the participants at Mass are also explained. Emphasis is placed on the real presence of Jesus in the Blessed Sacrament. As we are commissioned at the dismissal of every Mass, the children commit themselves to answering Jesus' call to share God's love with others.

Plan & Preview

▶ You might want to obtain children's scissors to help your child cut out the beautiful prayer cards on each family page of this unit.

▶ You might want a sheet of drawing or construction paper and markers to make the family peace agreement. *(Chapter 19 Family Page)*

Media Matters

Your child will be learning more about the Mass in this unit. Think back to last Sunday's Mass and how the priest said at dismissal, "Go in peace to love and serve the Lord." Take a news magazine or newspaper and cut out articles that show people loving and serving the Lord. Share these with your child. This is a wonderful way to balance the more depressing or even frightening news children see every day on TV.

Eucharistic Blessing

How holy this feast
in which Christ is our food:
his passion is recalled,
grace fills our hearts,
and we receive a pledge of the
glory to come.

Thomas Aquinas

Jesus Gives Us the Eucharist

15

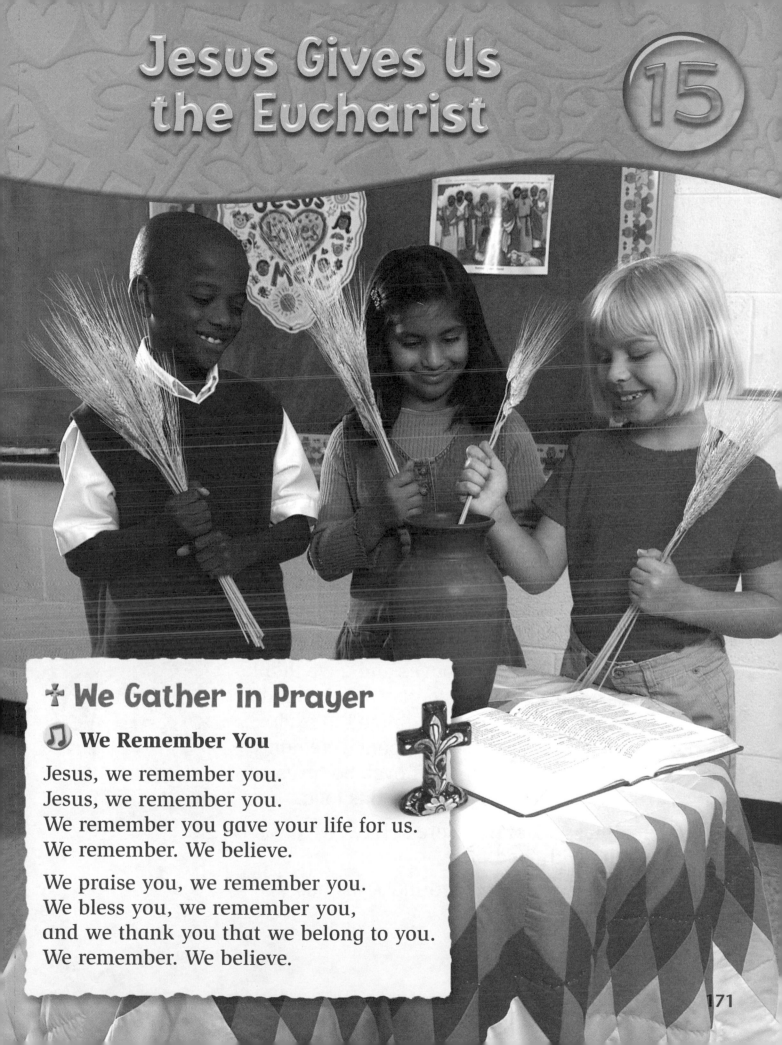

✝ We Gather in Prayer

♫ We Remember You

Jesus, we remember you.
Jesus, we remember you.
We remember you gave your life for us.
We remember. We believe.

We praise you, we remember you.
We bless you, we remember you,
and we thank you that we belong to you.
We remember. We believe.

171

Jesus brings us life.

WE GATHER

✝ *Jesus, you give us all we need.*

What kind of food do people make with wheat? Why is this food important?

WE BELIEVE

Act out the following story. It tells about a time when Jesus fed many hungry people.

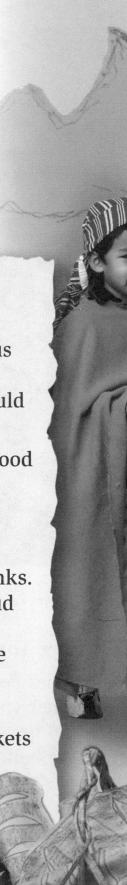

📖 John 6:2–14

Reader: One day thousands of people were listening to Jesus. He saw that the sun was setting. He knew that the people were hungry. Jesus asked Philip where they could find enough food for all these people.

Philip: Jesus, we could never find enough food to feed this many people!

Andrew: There is a boy here who has five loaves of bread and two fish.

Reader: Jesus took the loaves and gave thanks. He asked his disciples to give out the bread and fish. There was enough food to feed everyone. And when the people were done eating, there was food left over. So Jesus asked the disciples to gather this food.

Disciples: Look, there are still twelve baskets filled with food!

All: What a wonderful thing Jesus has done for us!

Jesus told us, "I am the living bread that came down from heaven; whoever eats this bread will live forever." (John 6:51)

All of us need bread to live and grow. All of us need Jesus to grow closer to God and share in God's life. Jesus is the living bread. He is the Son of God who was sent to bring us life.

WE RESPOND

How can we grow closer to Jesus? How can we help others to grow closer to Jesus?

Pray to Jesus and ask him to help you to grow closer to God.

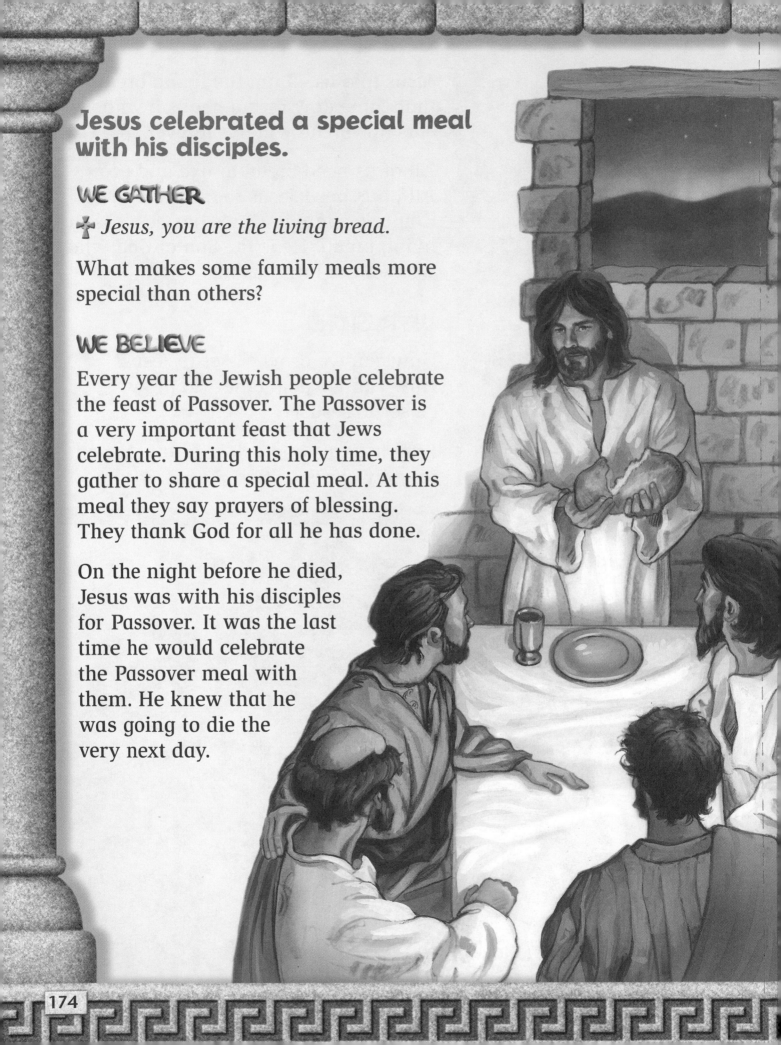

Jesus celebrated a special meal with his disciples.

WE GATHER

✟ *Jesus, you are the living bread.*

What makes some family meals more special than others?

WE BELIEVE

Every year the Jewish people celebrate the feast of Passover. The Passover is a very important feast that Jews celebrate. During this holy time, they gather to share a special meal. At this meal they say prayers of blessing. They thank God for all he has done.

On the night before he died, Jesus was with his disciples for Passover. It was the last time he would celebrate the Passover meal with them. He knew that he was going to die the very next day.

Here is what happened at the meal.

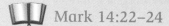 Mark 14:22–24

During the meal Jesus took bread and said a blessing. He broke the bread and gave it to his disciples. He said, "Take it; this is my body." (Mark 14:22)

Then Jesus took a cup of wine and gave thanks. All the disciples drank from this cup. Jesus said, "This is my blood." (Mark 14:24)

The meal Jesus shared with his disciples on the night before he died is called the **Last Supper**. At this meal the bread and wine became the Body and Blood of Jesus Christ.

Last Supper the meal Jesus shared with his disciples on the night before he died

Fill out this chart to help you remember what Jesus said and did at the Last Supper.

Jesus' Actions	Jesus' Words

WE RESPOND

Why was the Last Supper a special meal?

As followers of Jesus, when do we share special meals together?

In the Eucharist we remember and celebrate what Jesus did at the Last Supper.

WE GATHER

✝ *Jesus, thank you for giving yourself to us.*

What are some special events that you remember? Why does remembering them make you happy?

WE BELIEVE

At the Last Supper Jesus told the disciples to remember what he had just done. Jesus wanted them to remember and celebrate this special meal again and again. Jesus said, "Do this in memory of me." (Luke 22:19)

The Church continues to remember and celebrate what Jesus did at the Last Supper. We do as Jesus asked when we celebrate the Eucharist.

The **Eucharist** is the sacrament of the Body and Blood of Jesus Christ. In this sacrament, the bread and wine become the Body and Blood of Christ.

Key Word

Eucharist the sacrament of the Body and Blood of Jesus Christ

This is done by the power of the Holy Spirit and through the words and actions of the priest.

The word *eucharist* means "to give thanks." When we celebrate this sacrament, we thank God the Father for his many gifts and blessings. We praise Jesus for all he has done for us. We ask the Holy Spirit to help us grow closer to God and others.

WE RESPOND

What gifts has God given to your class? How can your class thank God for these gifts?

Name gifts that God has given you. What can you do this week to show that you are thankful for God's gifts? Draw or write your answer.

The Mass is a meal and a sacrifice.

WE GATHER

✝ *Holy Spirit, help us grow closer to God.*

Act out each story. Tell what is different about the meals.

- Gema is late for soccer practice. She quickly eats a sandwich.

- It is Gema's dad's birthday. All of Gema's family are coming over to celebrate. They will have a birthday dinner.

WE BELIEVE

The celebration of the Eucharist is called the **Mass.** During the Mass we gather together to listen to God's word and receive the Body and Blood of Christ.

The Mass is a meal. During the Mass we remember what Jesus did at the Last Supper. The bread and wine become the Body and Blood of Christ. **Holy Communion** is receiving the Body and Blood of Christ. Holy Communion makes the life of God within us stronger.

The Mass is a sacrifice. A *sacrifice* is an offering of a gift to God. The word *offer* means "to give" or "to present." Jesus offered the greatest sacrifice of all time. He died on the cross to save us from sin and to bring us new life.

As Catholics...

Every Catholic church has an altar. At the altar the sacrifice of Jesus is made present.

The altar is a table and it reminds us of the table of the Last Supper. From this table we receive Jesus in Holy Communion.

Think about the church where your parish community gathers for Mass. Where is the altar? What does the altar look like?

At every Mass we remember Jesus' sacrifice. We remember that Jesus gave himself so that we might have life.

Key Words

Mass the celebration of the Eucharist

Holy Communion receiving the Body and Blood of Christ

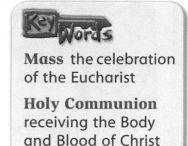

When we take part in the Mass, we remember and celebrate that:

- Jesus offered his life for us on the cross. He died to save us from sin.

- Jesus rose to new life so that we could live happily with God forever.

- Jesus gives us his own Body and Blood in Holy Communion. He gives us himself.

WE RESPOND

Look at the pictures below. What can each picture help you to remember about the Mass?

Use the words in the box to complete the sentences.

remember	give thanks	Mass	sacrifice

1. The word *eucharist* means to

_____ .

2. The celebration of the Eucharist is called the

_____ .

3. Jesus wants us to _____ and celebrate what he did at the Last Supper.

4. The Mass is a _____ and a meal.

Write your answer.

5. What did Jesus do at the Last Supper?

_____

_____

ASSESSMENT

Find a creative way to share with others that the Mass is:

• a sacrifice • a meal • a memory of Jesus.

We Respond in Faith

Reflect & Pray

What do you remember and celebrate at Mass? Finish the prayer.

Jesus, at Mass I want to

_____

_____

Last Supper (p. 175)
Eucharist (p. 176)
Mass (p. 179)
Holy Communion (p. 179)

Remember

- Jesus brings us life.
- Jesus celebrated a special meal with his disciples.
- In the Eucharist we remember and celebrate what Jesus did at the Last Supper.
- The Mass is a meal and a sacrifice.

OUR CATHOLIC LIFE

Sharing with the Hungry

Catholics follow Jesus' example when they help feed the hungry in their communities and the world. Many parishes sponsor food collections. Some parish groups give their time to make and serve meals in soup kitchens or homeless shelters. Some volunteers help people who are not able to leave their homes. These volunteers do grocery shopping. Sometimes they bring them prepared meals.

There are different ways you can help those who are hungry. You can pray for them. You can be careful not to waste food.

SHARING FAITH
with My Family

Sharing What I Learned

Look at the pictures below. Use each picture to tell your family what you learned in this chapter.

For All to See

"Do this in memory of me."
(Luke 22:19)

Grace Before Meals

As a family pray before meals. Make up your own prayer or pray the one below.

Bless us, O Lord, and these your gifts which we are about to receive from your goodness, through Christ, our Lord. Amen.

Celebrating a Family Meal

Make one of your family meals this week a special celebration. Together plan the menu and decorations.

Menu

_____

_____

Decorations

_____

_____

Visit Sadlier's

www.WeBelieveweb.com

 Connect to the Catechism
For adult background and reflection, see paragraphs 1406, 1339, 1341, and 1382.

✝ We Gather in Prayer

Leader: Join hands to form a circle. Let us listen to God's word.

Reader: Jesus said, "For where two or three are gathered in my name, there am I in the midst of them." (Matthew 18:20)

Leader: Jesus, we gather in your name. Together we thank God our Father for his many gifts.

All: God our Father, we thank you.

Leader: Jesus, we gather in your name. Together we praise you for all you have done for us.

All: God the Son, we praise you.

Leader: Jesus, we gather in your name. Together we ask the Holy Spirit to help us to grow closer to God and to others.

All: God the Holy Spirit, help us.

We are united to Jesus Christ and to one another.

WE GATHER

✝ *Jesus, we come together in your name.*

 Look at the picture of the grapevine. Circle where each branch is joined to the vine. Trace the way the food and water from the soil get to each of the branches.

WE BELIEVE

At the Last Supper, Jesus talked to his disciples about many things. One thing he told them was that he would always be with them.

Jesus also told them to stay close to him and to one another. He said, "I am the vine. You are the branches." (John 15:5) He told them that they were joined to him and one another as branches are joined to a vine.

Jesus wanted his disciples to work and pray together. He wanted them to share God's love with the whole world.

We are Jesus' disciples, too. Jesus is with us always. Each time we come together to celebrate the sacraments, he is with us. When we celebrate the sacrament of the Eucharist, Jesus is with us in a special way. He gives himself to us. We receive the bread and wine that have become the Body and Blood of Christ. We who receive Holy Communion are united to Jesus and to one another. Jesus is the vine and we are the branches.

WE RESPOND

How can you stay close to Jesus? How can you share God's love with your family, friends, and the world?

Join hands and pray together. Jesus, you are the vine. We are the branches. You give yourself to us as food in the Eucharist. Help us to grow in love for God and others.

The Church celebrates the Mass.

WE GATHER

✝ *Jesus, you are the vine and we are the branches.*

Why is Sunday a special day?

WE BELIEVE

Sunday is a special day for the Church. Sunday is also called the *Lord's Day*. This is because Jesus Christ rose to new life on this day. Every Sunday Catholics gather in their parishes. Together with their parish priest they celebrate the Mass.

The Mass is the greatest way to worship God. This is why the Church tells us to take part in the Mass every Sunday of the year. We can also celebrate the Sunday Mass on Saturday evening.

During Mass we gather as a community to:

• praise and thank God

• listen to God's word

• remember and celebrate Jesus' life, death, and resurrection

• celebrate Jesus' gift of himself in the Eucharist.

At the end of Mass we are sent out to live as Jesus taught us.

As Catholics...

One of the laws of the Church is that we must take part in the Mass every Sunday and on other special days. These other special days are called *holy days of obligation*. An obligation is a requirement.

In many places, Mass is celebrated each day of the week. We are invited to take part in Mass every day.

How does taking part in the Mass help us to live as Jesus taught us?

life

rose

👤 Find the words hidden in the picture.
Use these words to complete this sentence.

We call Sunday the

_____

because Jesus _____

to new _____ on this day.

WE RESPOND

How can you live Sunday as
the Lord's Day? How will
you share Jesus' love
this week?

The parish gathers for the celebration of Mass.

WE GATHER

✝ *God, we gather together to praise you.*

Name the people you usually see when your parish gathers to celebrate Mass.

WE BELIEVE

Many people come together for Mass. The community of people who join together for the celebration of the Mass is called the **assembly.** We are part of the assembly. The assembly gives thanks and praise to God throughout the whole celebration. A priest leads the assembly in this celebration.

Sometimes a deacon takes part in the celebration of the Mass. When a deacon is present, he reads the gospel during Mass. He prays some special prayers. He also helps the priest at the altar.

The priest offers our prayers to God. He does what Jesus did at the Last Supper.

Altar servers do many things to help the priest and deacon. Readers read the first two Bible readings. Special ministers of the Eucharist help give out Holy Communion.

Key Word

assembly the community of people who join together for the celebration of the Mass

After Mass, the special ministers of the Eucharist may bring Holy Communion to those who are sick or not able to be at Mass.

WE RESPOND

What can you do to participate at Mass now? What can you do to participate at Mass as you get older?

When Mass begins, we praise God and ask for his forgiveness.

WE GATHER

✝ *May the Lord be with us today.*

How do you take part in a special celebration?

WE BELIEVE

When we join together at Mass, we show God our love and thanks. It is important for each person in the assembly to take part in the celebration.

The beginning of the Mass unites us as members of the Church. It prepares us to hear God's word and to celebrate the Eucharist.

Here are the ways we take part as Mass begins.

- We greet other members of the community.

- We stand and sing to praise God as a community. As we sing, the priest, deacon, and others helping at Mass walk to the altar.

- We make the sign of the cross. This reminds us of our Baptism.

- The priest prays,
  "The Lord be with you."
  We respond,
  "And also with you."
  This helps us to know that Jesus is present with us.

- We ask God and one another for forgiveness.

- We ask for God's mercy. We pray with the priest:
  "Lord, have mercy.
  Christ, have mercy.
  Lord, have mercy."

- We sing or say together a prayer of praise. This prayer begins with these words.
  "Glory to God in the highest, and peace to his people on earth."

- The priest says an opening prayer. We respond,
  "Amen."

WE RESPOND

What are some ways you take part in the beginning of the Mass?

🎵 **God Is Here!**

God is here! Come, let us celebrate!
God is here! Let us rejoice!
God is here! Come, let us celebrate!
God is here! Let us rejoice!

Fill in the circle beside the correct answer.

1. As _____ we are joined to Jesus Christ and to one
   another.

   ○ members of the Church   ○ members of the school

2. Sunday is the Lord's Day because _____.

   ○ Jesus rose to new   ○ it is the best day
     life on this day   of the week

3. The _____ leads the assembly in Mass.

   ○ priest   ○ deacon

4. At the beginning of Mass, we _____.

   ○ receive Holy   ○ ask for God's
     Communion   forgiveness

5. Jesus is the vine and we are the branches. What
   does this mean?

   _____

   _____

ASSESSMENT

Begin to make a Mass booklet. Draw pictures
and write sentences to tell what we do as
Mass begins. You will add to your booklet in
the next three chapters.

We Respond in Faith

Reflect & Pray

Jesus promised that he would be with us always.

Jesus, _____

_____

_____

Key Word

assembly (p. 189)

Remember

- We are united to Jesus Christ and to one another.
- The Church celebrates the Mass.
- The parish gathers for the celebration of Mass.
- When Mass begins, we praise God and ask for his forgiveness.

OUR CATHOLIC LIFE

Welcome to the Celebration

In many parishes there are people who welcome us to the celebration of Mass. These people greet us as we enter the church. Their words help us to feel welcome and to know that we belong to the Church.

We should greet one another, too. Greeting one another is a good way to prepare for the celebration of the Eucharist.

SHARING FAITH
with My Family

Sharing What I Learned

Look at the pictures below. Use each picture to tell your family what you have learned in this chapter.

For All to See

"I am the vine, you are the branches."
(John 15:5)

Jesus, Help Us

Jesus, help us stay close to you by the words we say and by the things we do.

Jesus, we will keep you close in our hearts when our family is together and when we are apart.

Growing Closer to Jesus

With your family, talk about what each of you has done this week to grow closer to Jesus. Write one thing on each leaf of the vine below.

Visit Sadlier's

www.WEBELIEVEweb.com

Connect to the Catechism
For adult background and reflection, see paragraphs 1348, 1368, 1389, and 2643.

We Celebrate the Liturgy of the Word

✝ We Gather in Prayer

Leader: Let us pray.

🎵 **Alleluia, We Will Listen**

Alleluia, alleluia,
  we will listen to your word.
Alleluia! Alleluia!
We will listen. Alleluia!

Reader: A reading from the holy
  Gospel according to Luke.

Jesus "journeyed from one town
and village to another, preaching
and proclaiming the good news
of the kingdom of God." (Luke 8:1)

The Gospel of the Lord.

All: Praise to you, Lord Jesus Christ.

JESUS SHARES GOOD NEWS WITH US

We listen to God's word during the Liturgy of the Word.

WE GATHER

✝ *O God, we will listen to your word.*

You know the words to some stories and songs. How did you learn these words?

> 👤 Unscramble these letters to complete this sentence.
>
> ### e g i l n s t i n
>
> Sometimes we learn by
>
> l _ _ _ _ _ n _ _ _ .

WE BELIEVE

The Mass has two main parts. The first main part of the Mass is the **Liturgy of the Word**. During the Liturgy of the Word, we worship God by listening to his word. We listen to readings from the Bible.

At Sunday Mass we usually hear three readings from the Bible. When we listen to these readings, we grow in faith. We hear about God's love for us. We learn ways to show our love for God and others.

God's word has always been an important part of the Church's worship. We hear God's word during the celebration of all the sacraments.

By listening to God's word, we learn to be better followers of Jesus. We can learn to care for one another. As we listen and learn, we can grow in God's love.

WE RESPOND

How can listening to the word of God help you grow in faith?

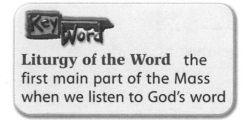 Work with a partner. Think of Bible stories that you remember. Tell the stories to one another. Talk about what each story means.

> **Key Word**
>
> **Liturgy of the Word** the first main part of the Mass when we listen to God's word

We listen and respond to readings from the Old Testament and the New Testament.

WE GATHER

✝ *O God, your ways are ways of love.*

What does your family do to remember the people and events that are special to all of you?

psalm a song of praise from the Bible

WE BELIEVE

The Liturgy of the Word begins with the first reading. The first reading is usually from the Old Testament. We hear about all the great things God did for his people before Jesus was born. This helps us to remember that God has always been with his people. When we listen, we also know that God is with us now.

After the first reading we let God's word enter our hearts. Then we sing a psalm. A **psalm** is a song of praise from the Bible. The leader of song or the reader prays a psalm verse. Then we sing or say a response.

Next we listen to the second reading. This is from the New Testament. It is about the teachings of the apostles and the beginning of the Church.

The way of the Lord

The way of the Lord

When we listen to the second reading, we learn how to be followers of Jesus. We remember and give thanks that we are the Church.

At the end of the first and second readings, the reader says, "The word of the Lord." We respond, "Thanks be to God."

WE RESPOND

What can you do during the week to prepare for the readings at Mass?

♫ Make up a tune or special beat for this psalm response.

"Your ways, O Lord, are love and truth."

Sing or say these words often.

We listen as the gospel is proclaimed.

WE GATHER

✝ *Praise to you, Lord Jesus Christ.*

We share good news with one another in a joyful way.

🏃 Act out how you would share this news.

- Grandfather is better. He is coming home from the hospital.
- Gabriella won first prize at the science fair.

WE BELIEVE

There are four books in the New Testament called gospels: Matthew, Mark, Luke, and John. In these gospels we learn the good news about Jesus' life and teaching. The third reading of the Liturgy of the Word is from one of the gospels.

The deacon or priest proclaims the gospel. To proclaim the gospel means to announce the good news of Jesus Christ with praise and glory.

Alleluia!

This is what we do:

- We stand. We sing the alleluia or other words of praise. This shows we are ready to listen to the good news of Jesus.

- We listen as the deacon or priest proclaims the gospel.

- Then the deacon or priest says, "The Gospel of the Lord." We respond, "Praise to you, Lord Jesus Christ."

After the gospel, the priest or deacon talks about the readings at Mass. In this talk he helps us to understand the readings. This talk is called the **homily**. Through the homily we learn what it means to believe and what we can do to be followers of Jesus. We learn how we can grow closer to God and to one another.

WE RESPOND

These are a few gospel stories that we have shared in class. Talk about each story.

- Jesus tells the story of the lost sheep (Luke 15:1–7).

- Jesus invites people to follow him (Matthew 4:18–22).

- Jesus tells the story of the forgiving father (Luke 15:11–24).

 Draw a ☺ beside the story you like best. Tell why you like it.

homily the talk given by the priest or deacon that helps us understand the readings and how we are to live

Together we pray the creed and the prayer of the faithful.

WE GATHER

✝ *God, we believe in you.*

🎵 We Believe

We believe in God the Father,
We believe in God the Son,
We believe in God the Spirit;
God is three, and God is one.

WE BELIEVE

After the homily we stand to pray the creed. In this prayer we show our faith. We say what we believe as Christians.

The word *creed* comes from a word that means "believe." Here are some of the words we say in the creed.

- "We believe in one God,
      the Father, the Almighty,
  maker of heaven and earth. . . ."

- "We believe in one Lord, Jesus Christ,
      the only Son of God. . . ."

- "We believe in the Holy Spirit, the Lord,
      the giver of life. . . ."

We also say that we believe in the Church and in God's forgiveness of our sins.

After the creed, we pray for the needs of all God's people. This prayer is called the prayer of the faithful. During this prayer, we pray for:

- the whole Church
- the pope and bishops
- the world and all its leaders
- those who are sick or in need
- the people in our parish who have died
- people we know and for whom we want to pray
- ourselves and any needs we may have.

After each prayer, we ask God to hear our prayer.

WE RESPOND

Who would you like to pray for next Sunday at Mass?

Pray quietly for these people now.

Review

Find the words in Column B that tell about the prayers or reading in Column A. Draw lines to match them. One is done for you.

A

"Thanks be to God." •

1. the first reading •

2. the creed •

3. prayer of the faithful •

4. "Praise to you, Lord Jesus Christ." •

B

• A prayer in which we say what we believe as Christians

• A prayer in which we pray for the needs of others

• One of the stories from the Old Testament

• Our response to the gospel reading

• Our response to the first and second readings

5. Why is it very important for us to listen to the gospel?

_____

_____

ASSESSMENT Add to your Mass booklet. Draw a picture and write a sentence to tell about each reading and prayer of the Liturgy of the Word.

We Respond in Faith

Reflect & Pray

What do we do and say when we pray the creed?

_____

_____

_____

Key Words

Liturgy of the Word (p. 197)

psalm (p. 198)

homily (p. 201)

Remember

- We listen to God's word during the Liturgy of the Word.
- We listen and respond to readings from the Old Testament and the New Testament.
- We listen as the gospel is proclaimed.
- Together we pray the creed and the prayer of the faithful.

OUR CATHOLIC LIFE

Praying for World Leaders

Leaders of the world have great responsibilities. That is why it is important to pray for them. We pray together for them during the prayer of the faithful on Sunday. We can also pray for them at other times.

We pray that leaders of our nation and world will rule with fairness. We pray that they share their countries' riches with all of those who are poor or in need. We ask the Holy Spirit to help world leaders work out problems in a peaceful way.

SHARING FAITH
with My Family

Sharing What I Learned

Look at the pictures below. Use each picture to tell your family what you learned in this chapter.

For All to See

"I wait with longing for the LORD, my soul waits for his word."
(Psalm 130:5)

We Pray for Others

Lead your family in this prayer. Have them say "Lord, hear our prayer" after each part of the prayer.

For the whole Church,
For all the people in our parish,
For those who are sick or in need,

Add your own.

Tips for Good Listeners

- Look at the person who is speaking.
- Pay close attention to what the speaker is saying.
- Picture in your mind what the speaker is talking about.

Discuss how these tips can help your family, especially the next time you listen to the readings at Mass.

Visit Sadlier's
www.WEBELIEVEweb.com

 Connect to the Catechism
For adult background and reflection, see paragraphs 1349 and 197.

✝ We Gather in Prayer

Leader: Write your initials in each gift box to show that you offer God all that you think, say, and do.

Now stand and lift up your books. Echo each line of the prayer.

We lift our minds and hearts in prayer. (Echo)

God, we offer to you today (Echo)

All we think, and do, and say, (Echo)

Uniting it with what was done (Echo)

On earth by Jesus Christ, your Son. (Echo)

We bring forward the gifts of bread and wine.

WE GATHER

✝ *God, we offer you all that we think and do and say.*

Justin's Aunt Sara gave him an art kit for his birthday. He used the crayons from the kit to make her a thank-you card.

Why was this a good way for Justin to thank his aunt?

WE BELIEVE

The **Liturgy of the Eucharist** is the second main part of the Mass. During the Liturgy of the Eucharist we present the gifts of bread and wine. A very special prayer is prayed. The bread and wine become the Body and Blood of Christ. We receive the Body and Blood of Christ.

We begin the Liturgy of the Eucharist by preparing the altar. This is also the time when we give money or other gifts for the Church and the poor. Ushers or other members of the assembly collect these gifts.

As Catholics...

The Church uses a special plate and cup at Mass. The plate is called a *paten*. The paten holds the bread that will become the Body of Christ. The cup is called a *chalice*. The chalice holds the wine that will become the Blood of Christ.

The next time you are at Mass, notice the paten and chalice.

Key Word

Liturgy of the Eucharist
the second main part of the Mass in which the gifts of bread and wine become the Body and Blood of Christ

Then members of the assembly bring forward the gifts of bread and wine. During this time we may sing a song. We remember that everything we have is a gift from God. We will offer these gifts and ourselves back to God.

The priest prepares these gifts of bread and wine with special prayers. We can respond: "Blessed be God for ever."

Then we are all invited to pray that the Lord will accept these gifts.

WE RESPOND

How can we show God we are thankful for his gifts?

🎵 A Gift From Your Children

Here is our gift, the bread and the wine:
A symbol of sharing, a beautiful sign:
A gift, a gift from your children;
A gift, a gift of our love.

Here is our gift, the song that we sing:
Raising our voices, praising your name!
Here is our gift, the song of our heart:
A gift, a gift of our love.

The eucharistic prayer is the great prayer of thanks and praise.

WE GATHER

✝ *Holy, holy, holy, Lord*

What are some different ways to show your thanks to others?

WE BELIEVE

After the preparation of the gifts, we pray the most important prayer in the Mass. This prayer is called the **eucharistic prayer**. It is the great prayer of praise and thanksgiving. This prayer is prayed in our name by the priest.

During this prayer we pray for many things. We lift up our hearts to the Lord. We remember all the things God has done for us. We praise God by singing "Holy, holy, holy. . . ." We call on the power of the Holy Spirit. We remember what Jesus said and did at the Last Supper.

The priest takes the bread. He says the words that Jesus said at the Last Supper. "Take this, all of you, and eat it: this is my body which will be given up for you."

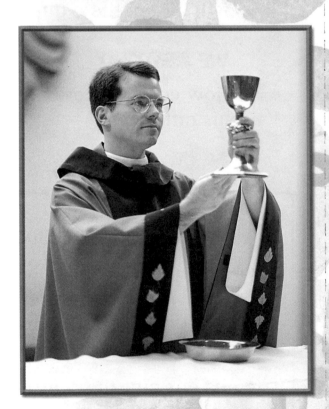

Then the priest takes the cup of wine. He says:
"Take this, all of you, and drink from it: this is the cup of my blood. . . ."

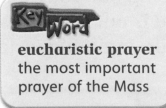

eucharistic prayer
the most important prayer of the Mass

210

This part of the eucharistic prayer is called the consecration. By the power of the Holy Spirit and through the words and actions of the priest, the bread and wine become the Body and Blood of Christ.

What looks like bread and tastes like bread is not bread anymore. What looks like wine and tastes like wine is not wine anymore. The bread and wine have become the Body and Blood of Christ. As Catholics we believe that Jesus Christ is really present in the Eucharist.

The priest invites us to proclaim our faith.

Write the word *Christ* at the beginning of each line.

_____ has died,

_____ is risen,

_____ will come again.

We pray that the Holy Spirit will unite all those who believe in Jesus.

We end the eucharistic prayer by responding "Amen." When we pray this word, we are saying "Yes, I believe." We are saying "yes" to the prayer the priest has prayed in our name.

WE RESPOND

Talk about what happens during the eucharistic prayer.

How can we show that we believe in Jesus?

211

We pray the Our Father and ask God for forgiveness and peace.

WE GATHER

✝ *Jesus, we believe in your presence.*

Use your own words to write one thing we pray for when we pray the Our Father.

_____

_____

WE BELIEVE

After the eucharistic prayer, we prepare to receive the Body and Blood of Christ. We join ourselves with the whole Church. We pray aloud or sing the Our Father.

After the Our Father, the priest reminds us of Jesus' words at the Last Supper. Jesus said, "Peace I leave with you; my peace I give to you." (John 14:27) We pray that Christ's peace may be with us always. We turn to the people who are near us and offer them a sign of peace. This action shows that we are all one. We are united to Christ and to one another.

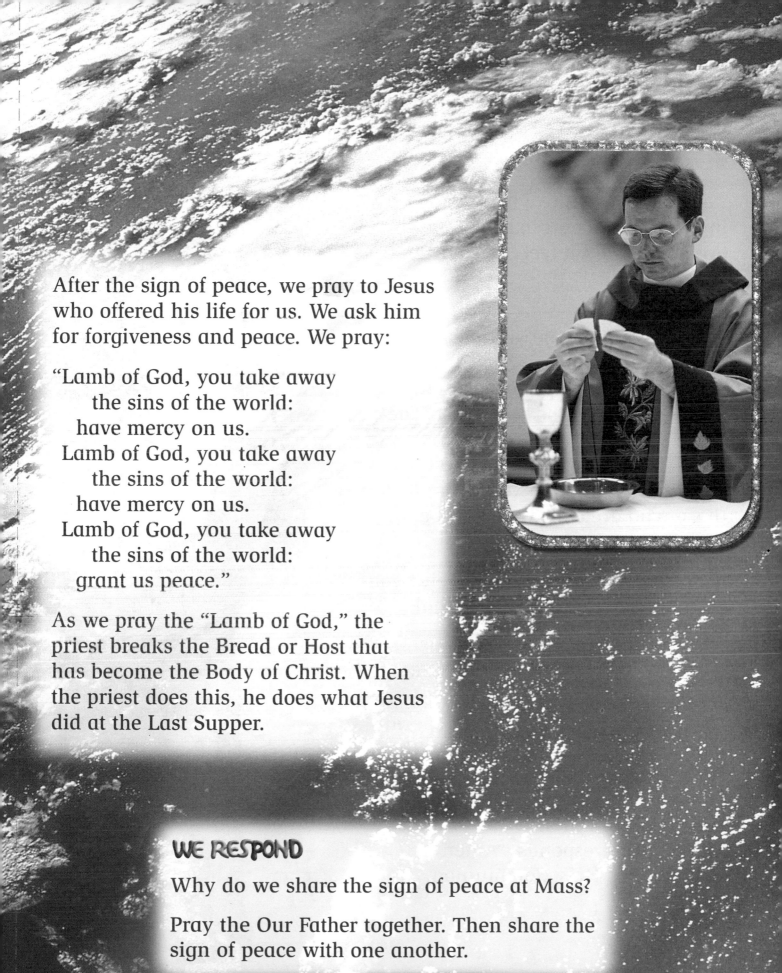

After the sign of peace, we pray to Jesus who offered his life for us. We ask him for forgiveness and peace. We pray:

"Lamb of God, you take away
   the sins of the world:
  have mercy on us.
 Lamb of God, you take away
   the sins of the world:
  have mercy on us.
 Lamb of God, you take away
   the sins of the world:
  grant us peace."

As we pray the "Lamb of God," the priest breaks the Bread or Host that has become the Body of Christ. When the priest does this, he does what Jesus did at the Last Supper.

WE RESPOND

Why do we share the sign of peace at Mass?

Pray the Our Father together. Then share the sign of peace with one another.

We receive Jesus Christ in Holy Communion.

WE GATHER

✝ *Jesus, you are the Lamb of God.*

Think about a time when you were invited to take part in an important event. How did it feel to be part of this?

WE BELIEVE

After we pray "Lamb of God," we are invited to share in the Eucharist. The priest holds up the Host that has become the Body of Christ. The priest says,
"This is the Lamb of God who takes away the sins of the world. Happy are those who are called to his supper."

We respond,
"Lord, I am not worthy to receive you, but only say the word and I shall
   be healed."

If we have received first Holy Communion, we go forward to receive the Body and Blood of Christ. The priest or special minister of the Eucharist shows the Host to each person who goes forward and says,
"The body of Christ."
Each person responds, "Amen" and receives Holy Communion.

Then the priest or special minister of the Eucharist may hand the cup to each person saying,
"The blood of Christ."
Each person responds, "Amen" and drinks from the cup.

While the assembly receives Holy Communion, we all sing a song of thanksgiving. We are united with one another.

Then there is usually some quiet time. During this time we remember Jesus is present within us. We thank Jesus for the gift of himself in Holy Communion.

WE RESPOND

What can you do to thank Jesus for the gift of himself in the Eucharist?

🎵 Jesus, You Are Bread for Us

Jesus, you are bread for us.
Jesus, you are life for us.
In your gift of Eucharist
  we find love.

When we feel we need a friend,
  you are there with us, Jesus.
Thank you for the friend you are.
Thank you for the love we share.

Review

Fill in the circle beside the correct answer.

1. The second main part of Mass is the _____.

   ○ Our Father   ○ Liturgy of the Eucharist

2. Bread and wine become the Body and Blood of Christ during the _____.

   ○ Our Father   ○ eucharistic prayer

3. We begin the Liturgy of the Eucharist by _____.

   ○ preparing the altar   ○ singing Amen

4. After we pray the _____, we are invited to share in the Eucharist.

   ○ Lamb of God   ○ Holy, holy, holy

5. Why is the eucharistic prayer the most important prayer of the Mass?

   _____

   _____

   _____

ASSESSMENT Add to your Mass booklet. Draw a picture and write a sentence to tell what happens during the Liturgy of the Eucharist.

We Respond in Faith

Reflect & Pray

Write a prayer to Jesus about receiving him in Holy Communion.

_____

_____

_____

Liturgy of the Eucharist (p. 209)
eucharistic prayer (p. 210)

Remember

- We bring forward the gifts of bread and wine.
- The eucharistic prayer is the great prayer of thanks and praise.
- We pray the Our Father and ask God for forgiveness and peace.
- We receive Jesus Christ in Holy Communion.

OUR CATHOLIC LIFE

First Holy Communion

The time when people are preparing to receive their first Holy Communion is very special. During this time, they learn about Jesus Christ and about the celebration of the Mass. They pray to God and live as followers of Jesus.

It is important for the people of the parish to pray for those preparing to receive first Holy Communion. In some parishes people volunteer to be prayer partners with them.

SHARING FAITH
with My Family

Sharing What I Learned

Look at the pictures below. Use each picture to tell your family what you learned in this chapter.

For All to See

"This is my body, which will be given for you."
(Luke 22:19)

Our Prayer to Jesus

Together write a prayer to thank Jesus for the gift of the Eucharist.

_____

_____

_____

_____

_____

Our Gift to God

Discuss with your family why it is an honor to bring the gifts to the altar at Mass.

Connect to the Catechism
For adult background and reflection, see paragraphs 1350, 1353, 1355, and 1386.

We Go in Peace to Share God's Love

19

✝ We Gather in Prayer

Leader: Let us listen to what Jesus told his disciples at the Last Supper.

Reader: Jesus said, "As I have loved you, so you also should love one another. This is how all will know that you are my disciples, if you have love for one another." (John 13:34–35)

Group 1: When we show respect for all people,

All: Jesus, we do as you asked.

Group 2: When we are kind and helpful,

All: Jesus, we do as you asked.

Group 3: When we forgive others,

All: Jesus, we do as you asked.

All: Jesus, help us to share your love and peace with others.

Amen.

We are sent to share God's love with others.

WE GATHER

✝ *Jesus, may we follow your loving ways.*

 What happens in your classroom at the end of your school day? Show what you say and do.

WE BELIEVE

The first disciples were sent out to continue Jesus' work. We are also disciples. Jesus asks us to continue his work, too.

The word *Mass* comes from a word that means "sending out." At the end of every Mass, the priest sends us out to share God's love with others.

Before we are sent out, the priest blesses us. We make the sign of the cross as he says,

"May almighty God bless you, the Father, and the Son, ✝ and the Holy Spirit."

We respond, "Amen."

Then the deacon or priest sends us to share God's love with others. He says, "Go in peace to love and serve the Lord."

We respond, "Thanks be to God."

WE RESPOND

How can you be a disciple of Jesus
and share his love with your family?
with people in your school?
with people in your neighborhood?

🎵 **Take the Word of God with You**

Take the peace of God with you
　　as you go.
Take the seeds of God's peace
　　and make them grow.

Go in peace to serve the world,
　　in peace to serve the world.
Take the love of God, the love of God
　　with you as you go.

221

Jesus is present in the Blessed Sacrament.

WE GATHER

✝ *Jesus help us to remember that you are with us always.*

Think about the church in your parish. Describe the inside of the church.

WE BELIEVE

After Holy Communion there may be Hosts that have not been received. These Hosts are called the Blessed Sacrament. The **Blessed Sacrament** is another name for the Eucharist.

The Blessed Sacrament is kept in the special place in the church called the **tabernacle.** There is always a special light or candle near the tabernacle. It helps us to remember that Jesus is really present in the Blessed Sacrament.

Key Words

Blessed Sacrament another name for the Eucharist

tabernacle the special place in the church in which the Blessed Sacrament is kept

After Mass and at other times, priests, deacons, and special ministers of the Eucharist take the Blessed Sacrament from the tabernacle. They bring the Blessed Sacrament as Holy Communion to those who are sick and to those who are not able to join the parish community for Mass. The Blessed Sacrament strengthens all those who receive it.

WE RESPOND

Jesus wants us to share God's love with those who are sick. We can do this by praying for them. We can also do this by visiting them or sending them get-well messages.

Design a card for someone who is sick. Tell them you are praying for them.

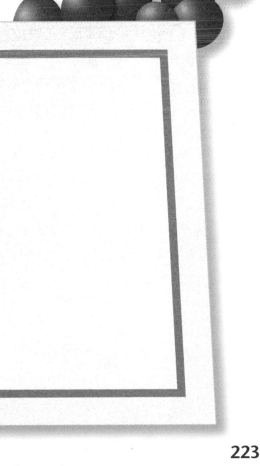

Jesus is with the Church as we share God's love.

WE GATHER

✝ *Jesus, help us to love and serve others as you did.*

Think about your good friends. How do other people know you are good friends?

WE BELIEVE

The early Christians were friends and followers of Jesus. They celebrated the Eucharist often. Receiving Jesus in the Eucharist helped their community. They were united with Jesus and one another. They were able to share God's love with others.

The early Christians learned and prayed together. They shared what they had with those who were poor and hungry. They tried to help those who were sad or lonely.

When people looked at the way the early Christians lived, they wanted to live as the Christians did. They wanted to become a part of Jesus' community, the Church.

please give

When we receive Jesus in Holy Communion, our friendship with him grows. Receiving Holy Communion helps us to love God and others. It helps us to be followers of Jesus. It helps us to be part of our parish. Together we show others what God's love is like.

Match the ways we can follow the example of the early Christians.

What the early Christians did	What we can do today
They fed those who were hungry. •	• We try to be calm and kind at home and in school.
They tried to live in peace with their families and others. •	• We pray with others. We take part in the Mass and celebrate the other sacraments.
They praised and thanked God often. •	• We collect food and clothing to give to those in need.

WE RESPOND

Who shows you what God's love is like? How?

What can you do together to share God's love in your parish? in your neighborhood?

Jesus is with us as we share his peace with others.

WE GATHER

✝ *Jesus, may we follow your peaceful ways.*

Look at the picture. What happens when you drop a pebble in water?

WE BELIEVE

During Mass we ask Jesus to give us peace. At the end of Mass, the deacon or priest tells us, "Go in peace." Jesus wants us to share his peace with others.

Every time we make a choice to be peaceful, we are like pebbles dropped in water. We spread Jesus' love and peace throughout the world.

WE RESPOND

Read the following stories. Draw a 💧 beside the peaceful choice.

• Mia and Carlos had a fight yesterday.

____ Mia thought, "I'm never going to talk to Carlos again."

____ Mia called Carlos. She said, "I'm sorry."

- Mrs. Pulski told the class, "We are going to learn about people in other countries. This may help us to live in peace with them."

____ Joseph thought, "Why do I have to learn about other countries? I don't care about people who live far away."

____ Joseph learned about the people of other lands. He shared what he learned with his family and friends.

- Cara's brother and sister are angry with each other.

____ Cara told her brother that their sister said something mean about him.

____ Cara told her brother and sister that they should make up with each other.

What are other ways to share Jesus' peace with others?

Pray these words quietly. When you see ◌, think about what you can do to share the peace of Jesus Christ.

Jesus, help us make peaceful choices. Help us to spread your peace and love

- in our homes ◌

- in our neighborhood ◌

- in our city or town ◌

- in the world ◌.

Write sentences to answer these questions.

1. What happens at the end of Mass?

_____

2. What is the Blessed Sacrament?

_____

3. What is the tabernacle?

_____

4. Name one way the early Christians shared God's love with others.

_____

Complete this sentence.

5. When we receive Holy Communion,

_____

_____

Complete your Mass booklet. Draw a picture and write a sentence that tells how you will go in peace to love and serve God and one another.

We Respond in Faith

Reflect & Pray

Jesus, thank you for the gift of the Eucharist. Thank you for

_____

_____

Blessed Sacrament (p. 222)

tabernacle (p. 222)

Remember

- We are sent to share God's love with others.
- Jesus is present in the Blessed Sacrament.
- Jesus is with the Church as we share God's love.
- Jesus is with us as we share his peace with others.

OUR CATHOLIC LIFE

Serving the Lord

Many people have shown us ways to "go in peace to love and serve the Lord." One person who did this was Saint Frances of Rome. Frances lived in the city of Rome, in Italy. She was married and had three children.

Frances took food to those who were poor in her city. She comforted the people who were sad and lonely. She cared for the children who had no families. Frances took care of the sick. She asked priests to visit those who wanted to celebrate Reconciliation and receive Holy Communion. Her feast day is March 9.

SHARING FAITH
with My Family

Sharing What I Learned

Look at the pictures below. Use each picture to tell your family what you learned in this chapter.

For All to See

"Peace I leave with you; my peace I give to you."
(John 14:27)

Praying for Peace
Gather together and pray as a family.

Jesus, help us to be peaceful.

Help us to spread your peace and love in our home, in our neighborhood, in our city or town, and throughout the world.

We pray that all families throughout the world may live in peace.

Family Peacemakers

Have a family meeting. Ask each member to discuss what he or she can do to make your home more peaceful. Together write a family peace agreement. Have each member sign it. Then post it for all to see.

Visit Sadlier's
www.WEBELIEVEweb.com

Connect to the Catechism
For adult background and reflection, see paragraphs 1332, 1397, 1416, and 1418.

Lent

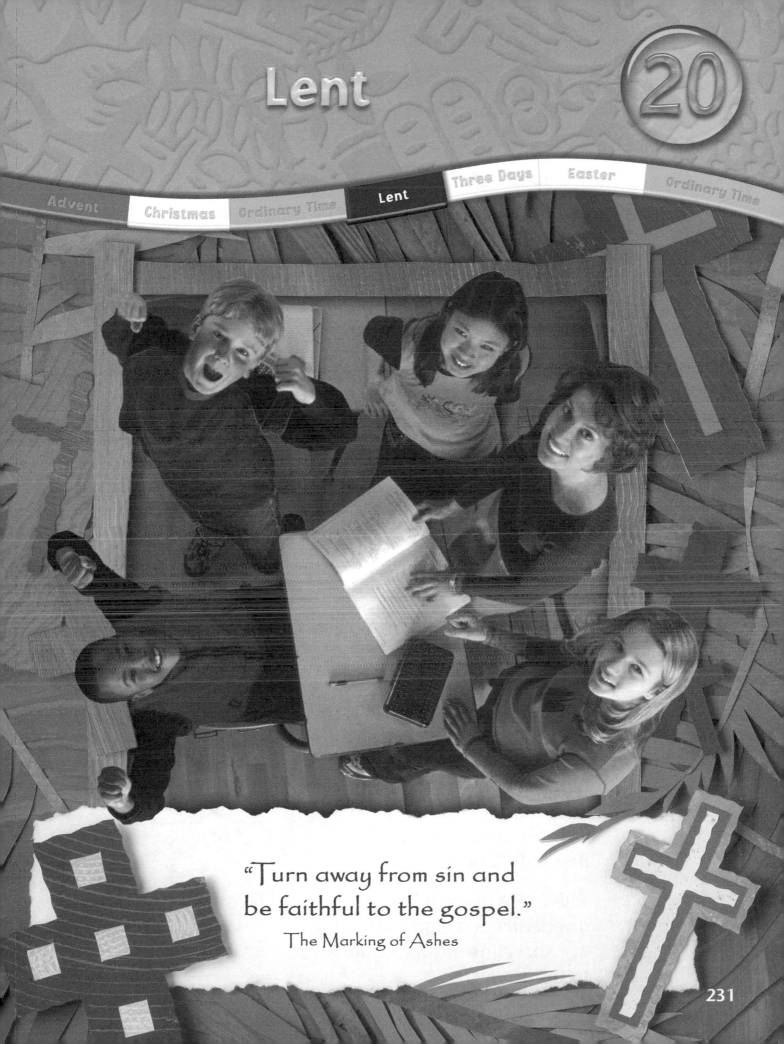

20

Advent Christmas Ordinary Time **Lent** Three Days Easter Ordinary Time

"Turn away from sin and
be faithful to the gospel."
The Marking of Ashes

231

Lent is a season of preparing.

WE GATHER

Sometimes a special logo or mark stands for something or someone. Think about some logos or marks that you know. What do they stand for?

WE BELIEVE

Lent is a time of remembering all that Jesus did to save us. It is a time to get ready. We get ready for the celebration of Easter and the new life that Jesus brings us.

The season of Lent lasts forty days. During that time we pray to God and ask for his forgiveness. We thank him for his mercy.

Lent begins on a day called Ash Wednesday. On Ash Wednesday, Catholics are marked with blessed ashes. The ashes are used to make a cross on our foreheads.

The cross reminds us that Jesus suffered and died for each of us. He did this so that we could live with God forever.

The cross of ashes on our foreheads is a sign that we are sorry for our sins and want to follow Jesus.

Lent is a time when we try to grow closer to Jesus. We follow Jesus by praying, doing good things for others, and helping the poor. We treat people with love and respect, the way Jesus did.

Look at the photos on this page.

Talk about the ways people are following Jesus.

WE RESPOND

The color of the season of Lent is violet or purple. On the chart, color the word *Lent*. During Lent, each time you show your love for God and others, draw a cross in one of these boxes.

LENT

✝ We Respond in Prayer

Leader: Loving God, open our ears and our hearts to the message of your Son.

Reader: A reading from the Gospel of Luke.

"Or what woman having ten coins and losing one would not light a lamp and sweep the house, searching carefully until she finds it? And when she does find it, she calls together her friends and neighbors and says to them, 'Rejoice with me because I have found the coin that I lost.' In just the same way, I tell you, there will be rejoicing among the angels of God over one sinner who repents." (Luke 15:8–10)

The Gospel of the Lord.

All: Praise to you, Lord Jesus Christ.

🎵 **We Are Yours, O Lord**

Help us to remember
who and what we are:
We are yours, O Lord.

SHARING FAITH
with My Family

Sharing What I Learned

Look at the pictures below. Use each picture to tell your family what you learned in this chapter.

The Giving Box

Find a special box or jar. During Lent, ask your family to think about people who are poor. Instead of spending money on treats or toys, put the money in the box or jar for people who are poor. With your family, choose a way to use this money to help people.

Our Lenten Prayer

Pray this prayer together often during Lent.

Jesus,
may we know you more clearly,
love you more dearly,
and follow you more nearly.

Amen.

(Saint Richard of Chichester)

Visit Sadlier's
www.WeBelieveweb.com

Connect to the Catechism
For adult background and reflection, see paragraph 540.

The Three Days

"We should glory in the cross
of our Lord Jesus Christ."

Evening Mass of the Lord's Supper

The Three Days celebrate the death and Resurrection of Jesus.

WE GATHER

Have you ever been to a celebration that lasted more than one day? What was it?

WE BELIEVE

During Lent we prepare to celebrate Jesus' death and Resurrection in a special way. When Lent ends, we begin the Three Days.

The Three Days are the Church's greatest celebration. They are the most important days of the Church year. During the Three Days, we gather with our parish. We gather to celebrate at night and during the day. The celebration of the Three Days begins on Holy Thursday evening and ends on Easter Sunday evening.

Trace over the lines to show when the Three Days begin and end.

DAY 1   **DAY 2**   **DAY 3**

| Holy Thursday | Good Friday | Holy Saturday | Easter Sunday |

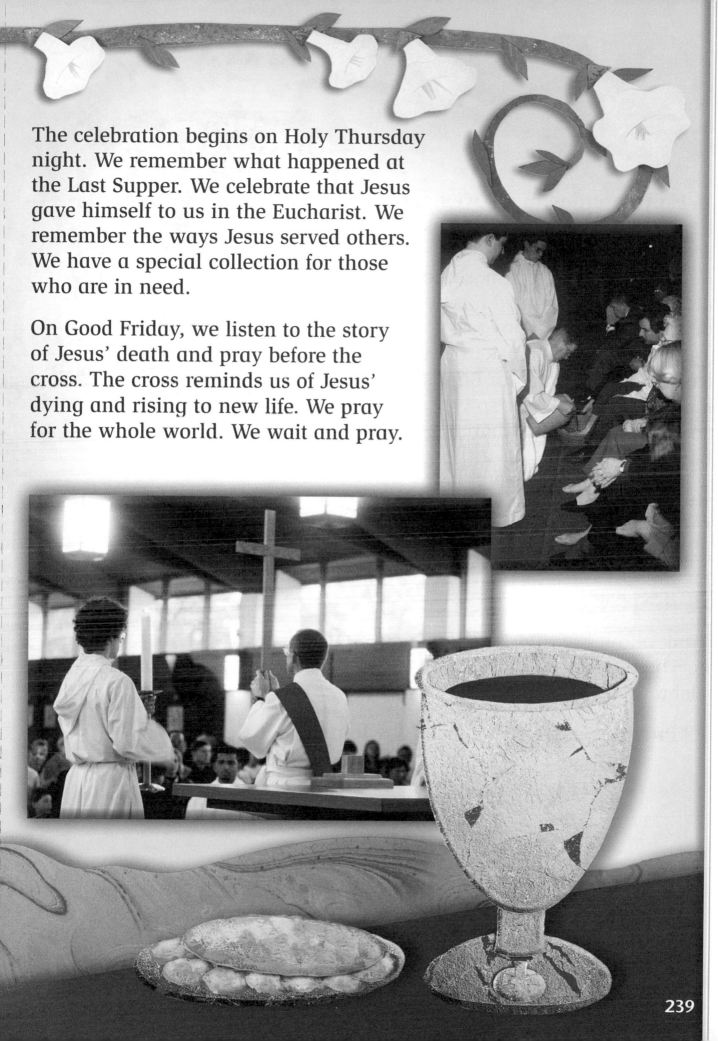

The celebration begins on Holy Thursday night. We remember what happened at the Last Supper. We celebrate that Jesus gave himself to us in the Eucharist. We remember the ways Jesus served others. We have a special collection for those who are in need.

On Good Friday, we listen to the story of Jesus' death and pray before the cross. The cross reminds us of Jesus' dying and rising to new life. We pray for the whole world. We wait and pray.

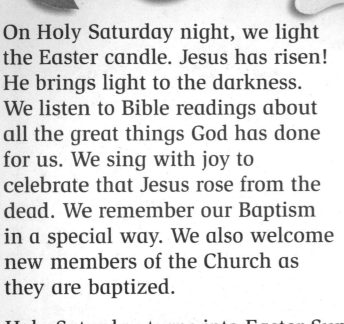

On Holy Saturday night, we light the Easter candle. Jesus has risen! He brings light to the darkness. We listen to Bible readings about all the great things God has done for us. We sing with joy to celebrate that Jesus rose from the dead. We remember our Baptism in a special way. We also welcome new members of the Church as they are baptized.

Holy Saturday turns into Easter Sunday. We sing songs of joy and praise as we begin the Easter season. Alleluia!

WE RESPOND

Think about the things we do to celebrate the Three Days. How does your parish celebrate the Three Days?

Pray this prayer. Then color the frame.

**Christ has died.
Christ is risen.
Christ will come again.**

✝ We Respond in Prayer

Leader: Rejoice in Jesus Christ always!

All: Rejoice in Jesus Christ always!

Reader: A reading from the Letter of Saint Paul to the Galatians.

"Through faith you are all children of God in Christ Jesus. For all of you who were baptized into Christ have clothed yourselves with Christ. You are all one in Christ Jesus." (Galatians 3:26, 27, 28)

The word of the Lord.

All: Thanks be to God.

🎵 **Alleluia, We Will Listen**

Alleluia, alleluia,
We will listen to your word.
Alleluia! Alleluia!
We will listen.
Alleluia!

THE THREE DAYS

SHARING FAITH
with My Family

Sharing What I Learned

Look at the pictures below. Use each picture to tell your family what you learned in this chapter.

Around the Table

The Church's celebration of the great Three Days begins on Holy Thursday evening and ends on Easter Sunday evening. See the calendar boxes below.

Mark these days on your family calendar. Talk together about ways your parish celebrates on these days.

DAY 1   **DAY 2**   **DAY 3**

| Holy Thursday | Good Friday | Holy Saturday | Easter Sunday |

The Three Days

For All to Pray

"We should glory in the cross of our Lord Jesus Christ."

Visit Sadlier's
www.WeBelieveweb.com

Connect to the Catechism
For adult background and reflection, see paragraph 628.

Circle the correct answer.

1. In the Eucharist we celebrate what Jesus did _____.

    at the Last Supper   during Lent

2. The first reading of the Mass is a story from the _____.

    Old Testament   New Testament

3. We receive the Body and Blood of Christ in _____.

    the homily   Holy Communion

4. At the beginning of the Mass, we gather as a community.

    Yes   No

5. Jesus is present in the Blessed Sacrament.

    Yes   No

6. The Mass is only a meal.

    Yes   No

7–8. Name two ways the early Christians loved and served others.

_____

_____

continued on next page

9–10. Name two ways you can love and serve others today.

_____

_____

Read the prayers and actions of the Mass below. In what part of the Mass does each belong? Write each in the correct column of the chart.

proclaim the gospel

eucharistic prayer

prepare the gifts of bread and wine

psalm response

sign of peace

the creed

Lamb of God

listen to the homily

receive Holy Communion

prayer of the faithful

Liturgy of the Word	Liturgy of the Eucharist
_____	_____
_____	_____
_____	_____
_____	_____
_____	_____

We Live Our Catholic Faith

UNIT 4 SHARING FAITH as a Family

Making Time for Family Meals

It is widely accepted that sitting down together to share a meal is a beneficial part of family life. It is also hard to do. Sports, work, and the rush hour commute all present obstacles to such gatherings. Nevertheless, many families are making mealtime a priority.

Here are some practical ways your family can do the same.

- Connect a special meal once a month to a family activity. Make a night of it!

- Designate a weekly "family favorite" night around a particular food, such as pizza, pasta, burgers, or burritos. The emphasis is on simplicity and generating anticipation for a meal everyone enjoys.

- Decide what *can't* be brought to the table. Sometimes families don't want to eat together because the time is spent arguing with or correcting each other. Placing emphasis on good conversation helps the digestion better than the best antacid!

- If dinner doesn't work, decide on another meal. Breakfast can be a delightful way for some, if not all, of the family to start the day.

In conclusion, don't forget that mealtimes can be ideal occasions for family prayer.

From the Catechism

"The *Christian family* is the first place of education in prayer."

(Catechism of the Catholic Church, 2685)

Bible Q & A

Q: When I was a child, I felt very close to Mary. How can I help my son to get to know her better? What verses should I read?
-Coventry, Rhode Island

A: To appreciate Mary more deeply, turn to Luke 1:26–38, John 2:1-11, and John 19:25–27.

God's Call

In this unit, your child will recognize that God calls each one of us to use our gifts of faith, hope, and love to serve others. Together, as a family, answer this call.

You can start by researching a service project in your parish or community that would be appropriate for your family. This might be sorting food in a food bank, or visiting shut-ins, etc. Once you have selected a project, meet as a family to discuss each family member's commitment and responsibilities (time, safety issues, tasks, etc.) Then go and serve!

Following your family's participation, ask each family member to share her or his personal experience of answering God's call to serve others.

What Your Child Will Learn in Unit 4

Unit 4 focuses on the ways that the children can live out their faith. They are first presented with the vocations of lay people, priests, and religious brothers and sisters. Focus is then directed from naming the local parish, diocese, and bishop to a clearer understanding of the Church throughout the world. The children will become more aware of what prayer is as well as how Jesus prayed. This leads to a presentation of the Our Father and ways we can pray. Unit 4 also offers the children an opportunity to learn more about Mary, the events in her life, her feast days, and the great prayer, Hail Mary. Examples of other saints are given as well as a commentary on feast days and popular devotions. Grade 2 is concluded with an inspiring summary of Jesus' new commandment and the Ten Commandments.

Plan & Preview

▶ The next time you are at your parish, obtain a copy of your diocesan newspaper. Most likely you receive it at home or can find an online version on your diocesan web site. *(Chapter 22 Family Page)*

▶ Have available a spiral notebook or a family journal. *(Chapter 24 Family Page)*

MY FAMILY JOURNAL

God Calls Us to Love and Serve

✝ We Gather in Prayer

Leader: God, our Father,
in Baptism you called us by name
making us members of your
people, the Church.

All: We praise you for your goodness.
We thank you for your gifts.

Leader: We ask you to strengthen us
to live in love and service to others as
your Son, Jesus, did.

We ask this through Christ,
our Lord.

All: Amen.

We are called by God.

WE GATHER

✝ *God, help us to show others your love.*

Think about a time when your parent called your name. What did you do when you heard your name called?

WE BELIEVE

We read in the Bible that God says, "I have called you by name: you are mine." (Isaiah 43:1)

When we are **called by God**, we are invited by God to love and serve him.

We love and serve God now in many ways. We do and say things to show our love for God.

As members of the Church we pray and respect God's name. We take part in the Mass and celebrate the other sacraments. We learn about God from the teachings of Jesus and the Church. We tell others the wonderful things God has done for us. These are some of the ways we love and serve God.

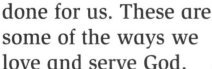

As we grow older we are called to serve God in different ways. We may serve God as single people, married people, priests, or religious brothers or sisters. These ways of serving God are all important to the Church. Together we work to bring God's love to others.

called by God invited by God to love and serve him

WE RESPOND

Complete the following chart.

People who serve God	What they do

What is one thing you can do to love and serve God this week?

Married people and single people are called by God.

WE GATHER

✝ *Jesus, show us the way to love one another.*

🏃 Family members have many ways to show love for one another. Make up a storyboard about a loving family.

WE BELIEVE

In our families there are single people and married people. They serve God in many of the same ways.

- They love and care for their families.
- They take part in parish activities.
- They tell others about Jesus and the Church.
- They work to make their communities better places.

Single people and married people also serve God by helping people who are in need. They spend time with people who are lonely. They visit people who are sick. They pray for others.

Single people serve God by serving others. They share God's love in their families, communities, and the Church.

Married people celebrate the sacrament of Matrimony. A husband and wife share God's love in special ways with each other and with their children. They teach their children about Jesus and the Church. They show them how to live as Catholics.

WE RESPOND

Tell about ways families can show love for God and others.

♫ God Has Made Us a Family

Chorus
God has made us a family
 and together we will grow in love.
God has made us a family
 and together we will grow in love.

Oh! Yes! We need one another,
 as together we grow in love;
and we will forgive one another,
 as together we grow in love. (Chorus)

Priests are called by God.

WE GATHER

✝ *God, thank you for your love.*

Name the priests who work in your parish.

WE BELIEVE

Some men are called, or invited, to serve God and the Church as priests. A man becomes a priest when he receives the sacrament of Holy Orders.

Priests spend their lives sharing God's love with people. Priests share the message of Jesus. They help us to live as Jesus did.

Priests lead the celebration of the Mass and other sacraments. They teach us about our Catholic faith. They work in parishes, schools, hospitals, and communities all over the world.

As Catholics...

During the sacraments, priests wear special clothing called vestments. The priest wears a long robe, called an alb, with a narrow scarf, called a stole, around his neck. He covers both of these with another vestment called a chasuble. The priest wears different colored chasubles at different times. The color tells us something about the Church season or feast being celebrated. Some of the colors you might see are purple, rose, white, red, green, and gold.

This Sunday at Mass look to see what color chasuble the priest is wearing.

WE RESPOND

Look at the pictures on these pages. How is each priest loving and serving God and others?

Draw a thank-you card for your parish priest. Thank him for all he does for God and others.

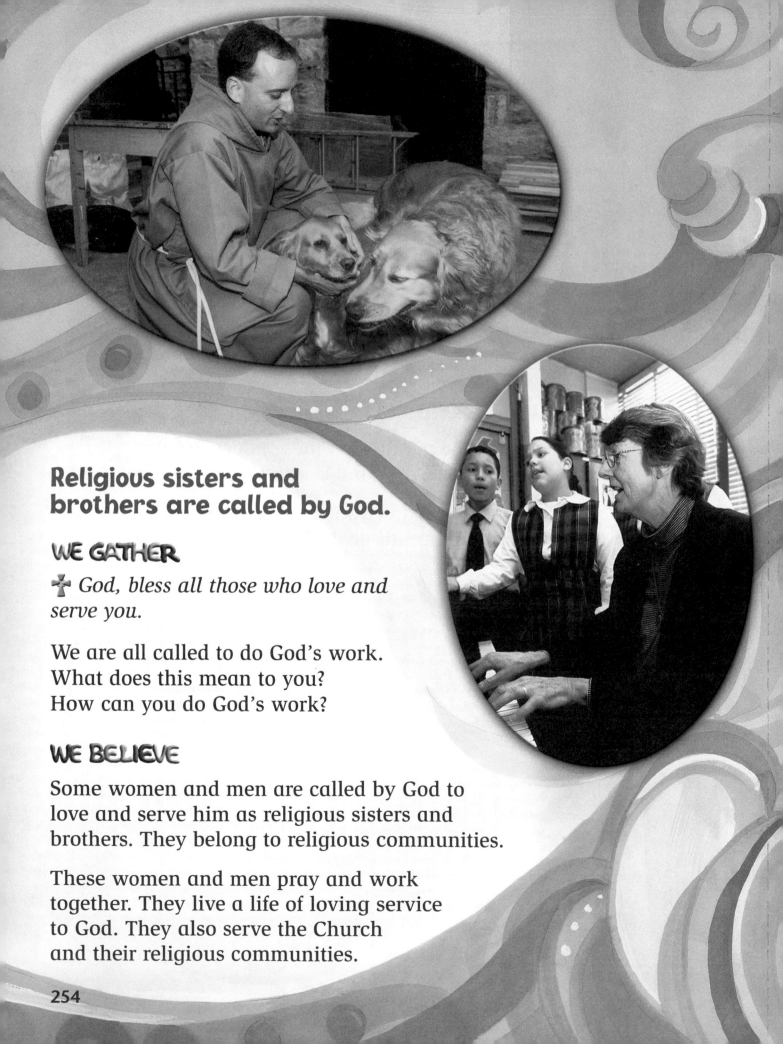

Religious sisters and brothers are called by God.

WE GATHER

✝ *God, bless all those who love and serve you.*

We are all called to do God's work. What does this mean to you? How can you do God's work?

WE BELIEVE

Some women and men are called by God to love and serve him as religious sisters and brothers. They belong to religious communities.

These women and men pray and work together. They live a life of loving service to God. They also serve the Church and their religious communities.

Religious sisters and brothers spend their lives sharing God's love with people. They serve in many ways.

- They can tell others about Jesus either in our country or in faraway places.

- They can teach in schools and parishes.

- They can work in hospitals and spend time with those who are sick or elderly.

- They can care for people who are poor or in need.

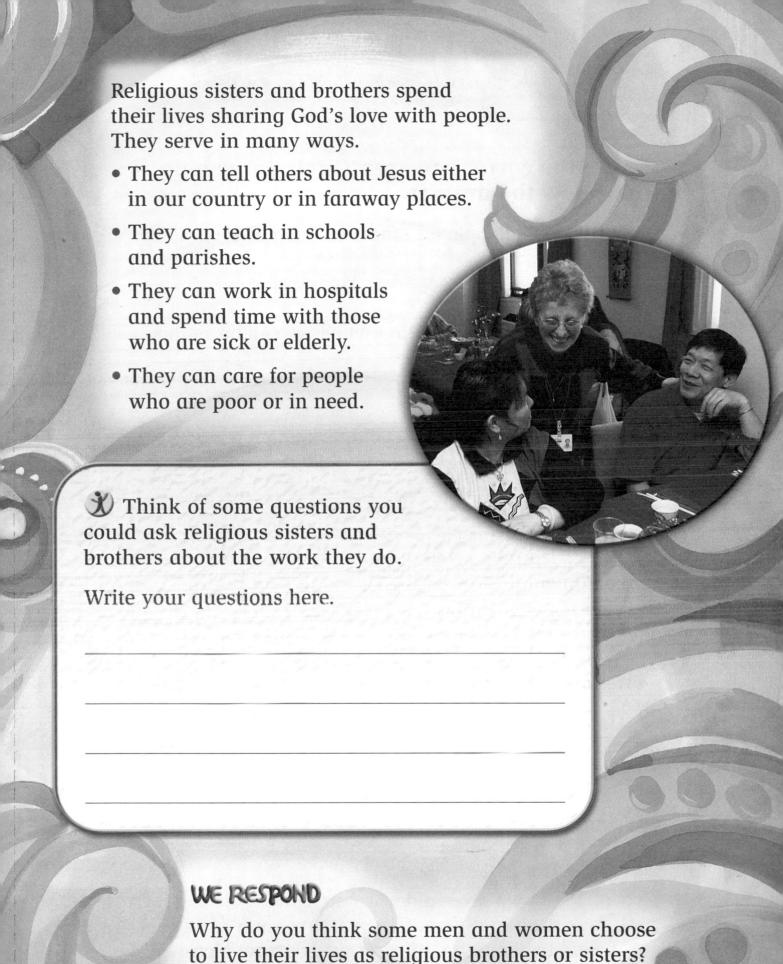

Think of some questions you could ask religious sisters and brothers about the work they do.

Write your questions here.

_____

_____

_____

_____

WE RESPOND

Why do you think some men and women choose to live their lives as religious brothers or sisters?

Circle the correct answer. Circle ? if you do not know the answer.

1. Only single people and married people serve God.

Yes   No   ?

2. We show our love for God when we celebrate the sacraments.

Yes   No   ?

3. Only women can belong to religious communities.

Yes   No   ?

4. Priests lead the celebration of the Mass and other sacraments.

Yes   No   ?

Answer this question.

5. How does the Church love and serve God?

_____

_____

As we grow older we are called to serve God in different ways. Make up a booklet to show the different ways. Draw pictures and write sentences.

We Respond in Faith

Reflect & Pray

God, I would like to serve you as

_____ .

Holy Spirit, help me

_____

_____ .

called by God (p. 249)

Remember

- We are called by God.
- Married people and single people are called by God.
- Priests are called by God.
- Religious sisters and brothers are called by God.

OUR CATHOLIC LIFE

Elizabeth Ann Seton

Saint Elizabeth Ann Seton is the first person from the United States to be named a saint. She was born in New York City and was baptized in the Episcopal Church. She married William Seton and had five children. After her husband died, she became a Catholic. She taught and helped the poor. She started the first Catholic school in the United States in Emmitsburg, Maryland. She also started a religious community, the Sisters of Charity. They still teach in schools, work in hospitals, and help in parishes today.

SHARING FAITH with My Family

Sharing What I Learned

Look at the pictures below. Use each picture to tell your family what you learned in this chapter.

For All to See

"First, I give thanks to my God, through Jesus Christ for all of you. . . ."

(Romans 1:8)

Read All About It

Many dioceses have weekly newspapers or Web sites. You can read about the ways married and single people, priests, and religious sisters and brothers serve God.

With your family find pictures and stories of people serving God and others. Talk about the ways they are serving.

Our Gift to God

As a family, write a letter to or send an e-mail to the editor of the newspaper. Thank the people you have read about for their love and service.

Visit Sadlier's

www.WeBelieveweb.com

Connect to the Catechism
For adult background and reflection, see paragraphs 30, 1578, 1604, 1618, and 1658.

The Church Lives Today

✝ We Gather in Prayer

Leader: Let us listen to a reading from the letter of Paul to the Philippians.

Reader: "Rejoice in the Lord always. I shall say it again: rejoice! Your kindness should be known to all."
(Philippians 4:4–5)

The word of the Lord.

All: Thanks be to God.

Leader: Together let us lift our voices in praise to the Lord.

♫ Rejoice in the Lord Always

Rejoice in the Lord always,
  Again I say, rejoice!
Rejoice in the Lord always,
  Again I say, rejoice!
Rejoice! Rejoice!
  Again I say, rejoice!
Rejoice! Rejoice!
  Again I say, rejoice! (Repeat)

Catholics belong to parish communities.

WE GATHER

✝ *God, help us as we try to do your work.*

You belong to a family. You also belong to your class at school. How are these groups the same? How are they different?

WE BELIEVE

As Catholics we also belong to a parish family. A parish is a community of Catholics who worship and work together.

As a parish, we come together to pray. We celebrate the sacraments. We care for those in need. We learn to live as followers of Jesus.

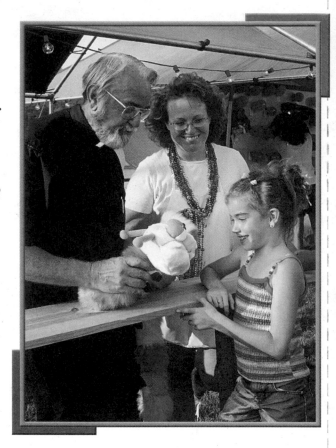

Read the sentences below. Put a check by each thing you can do to take part in your parish.

- ☐ Join the parish for Mass.

- ☐ Prepare to celebrate the sacraments.

- ☐ Help with food drives and other projects for those in need.

- ☐ Welcome others to my parish by being friendly.

- ☐ Sing or play an instrument in the children's choir.

- ☐ Attend special activities my parish holds for children and families.

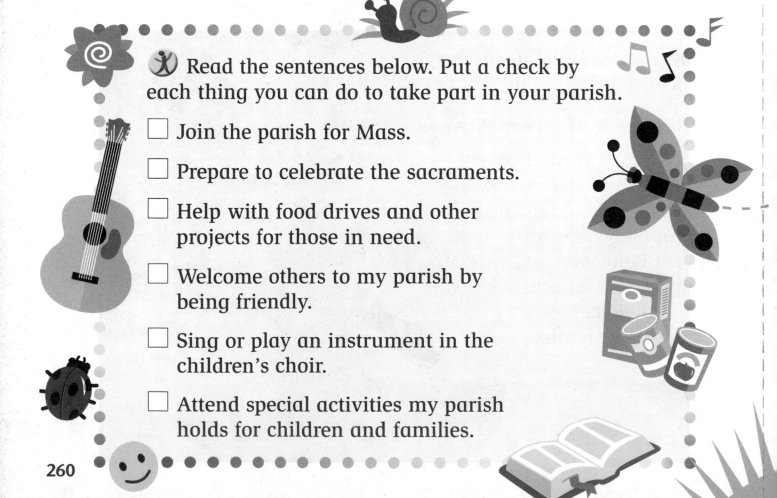

A parish has a pastor who is chosen by the bishop. The **pastor** is the priest who leads and serves the parish. He leads the parish in celebrating the sacraments, in prayer, and in teaching.

Together with the pastor, the members of the parish continue the work of Jesus. Some of these people help in parish ministries. Together the whole parish serves the needs of others, especially those who are poor, sick, or lonely.

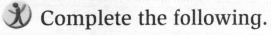

WE RESPOND

Complete the following.

I belong to _____ parish.

My pastor is _____.

In our parish we continue the work of Jesus

by _____

_____.

Bishops lead and serve the Church.

WE GATHER

✝ *Jesus, bless our parish community.*

Would you like to be the leader of a group you belong to? Why or why not?

What does a good leader do?

WE BELIEVE

Jesus chose the twelve apostles to lead and care for his followers. He chose the apostle Peter to be the leader of the apostles. Peter and the other apostles were the first leaders of the Church. They led the Church in continuing the work of Jesus.

Peter and the apostles chose other men to lead and serve the Church. These leaders became known as bishops. Bishops still lead and serve the Church today. **Bishops** are leaders of the Church who carry on the work of the apostles.

A bishop is chosen by the pope to lead and care for a diocese. A **diocese** is an area of the Church led by a bishop. A diocese is made up of all the Catholics who live in a certain area.

The bishop guides and serves the members of his diocese. He passes on the teachings of Jesus. He helps the people to grow closer to God.

Use the code. What are we part of?

A	C	D	E	H	I	O	P	R	S	U
1	2	3	4	5	6	7	8	9	10	11

A Catholic is part of a ___ ___ ___ ___ ___ ___,
               8   1   9   6   10   5

which is part of a ___ ___ ___ ___ ___ ___ ___,
          3   6   7   2   4   10   4

which is part of the ___ ___ ___ ___ ___ ___.
          2   5   11   9   2   5

WE RESPOND

What diocese is your parish part of? My parish is part of the diocese of

_____.

How can we show others that we are part of the Church?

The pope is the leader of the Church.

WE GATHER

✝ *Jesus, guide the leaders of the Church.*

🏃 Act out some things Saint Peter did to lead the Church.

WE BELIEVE

The pope is the bishop of Rome in Italy. The **pope** is the leader of the Church who continues the work of Saint Peter. With the other bishops, the pope helps Catholics to be disciples of Jesus.

The pope serves and cares for the Church. He preaches the good news of Jesus Christ to everyone. Wherever he is, the pope celebrates Mass and talks to the people.

The pope travels to other countries. The pope listens to the people's problems. He sees the good things they are doing for others. He asks them to love and care for one another. He teaches them about God's love and forgiveness.

Pope John Paul II greets people in Saint Peter's Square at Vatican City.

Key Word

pope the leader of the Church who continues the work of Saint Peter

As Catholics...

The pope lives in a special part of Rome called Vatican City. Vatican Radio sends out its programs in forty different languages so everyone who listens can understand. Every day the pope's messages and other programs about Jesus and the Catholic faith can be heard on Vatican Radio. Vatican Radio programming is broadcasted on the radio and over the Internet on the Vatican's own Web site at www.vatican.va.

Listen to the pope's message on Vatican Radio or log on to the Vatican's Web site.

WE RESPOND

If the pope were coming to your parish, what would you want to ask him?

_____

_____

What would you want to tell him?

_____

_____

The Church is in every part of the world.

WE GATHER

✝ *Holy Spirit, let us live in peace with all your people.*

Tell about some things your family does each year to celebrate holidays and birthdays.

WE BELIEVE

Catholics live in every part of the world. Catholics everywhere have the same beliefs.

These Catholics are Polish. It is Christmas Eve. The father of this Catholic family is breaking a wafer made of wheat called *oplatki (ō plát key)*. He will give a piece of the wafer to each member of his family. Sharing oplatki is a sign of love and peace.

These Catholics are celebrating the Feast of Corpus Christi, or the Feast of the Body and Blood of Christ. The priest is carrying the Eucharist for all to worship. The priest and people sing songs to Jesus as they walk through the streets of their town in a procession.

Catholics share and celebrate the same beliefs about the Blessed Trinity. They share the same beliefs about Jesus, the Son of God, the Church, Mary and the saints. They all celebrate the Eucharist and the other sacraments. They look to the pope as the leader of the Church.

However, Catholics around the world also show their faith in different ways.

Look at the pictures on these pages. Then read the sentences about each picture. You will learn some of the different ways Catholics pray and show their faith.

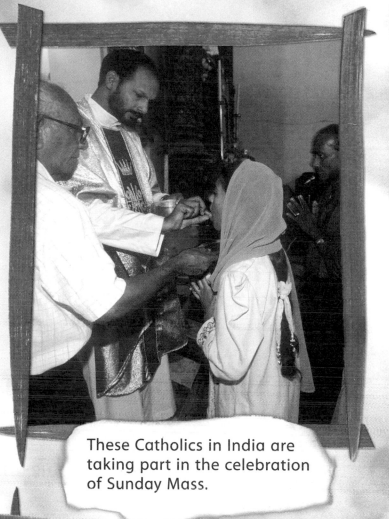

These Catholics in India are taking part in the celebration of Sunday Mass.

These Catholic children are honoring Mary in a special way during the month of May. They are placing a crown of flowers on a statue of Mary.

WE RESPOND

What could you tell a second grade class from another country about the way your parish prays and celebrates?

267

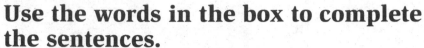

Use the words in the box to complete the sentences.

| pope | parish | members | faith | bishops |

1. A _____ is a community of Catholics who worship and work together.

2. The _____ lead the Church and carry on the work of the apostles.

3. The _____ is the leader of the Church who continues the work of Saint Peter.

4. The _____ of the parish continue the work of Jesus.

Write your answer.

5. Catholics share and celebrate

_____

_____

Make up a question for each of these answers: parish, people, pastor, diocese, bishop, and pope. Share your questions with a partner. Answer your partner's questions, too.

We Respond in Faith

Reflect & Pray

Jesus, the Church continues your work today

by _____

_____

_____

Please help me to continue your work.

Key Words

pastor (p. 261)
bishops (p. 263)
diocese (p. 263)
pope (p. 264)

Remember

- Catholics belong to parish communities.
- Bishops lead and serve the Church.
- The pope is the leader of the Church.
- The Church is in every part of the world.

OUR CATHOLIC LIFE

Missionaries

All of us are called to be missionaries. Missionaries teach others about Jesus. They follow Jesus' example. We can be missionaries within our homes, schools, and neighborhoods. We can share our belief in Jesus and live as he did.

Some missionaries bring the good news of Jesus Christ to people who live in other countries. Missionaries in other countries learn the local language. They also learn the way the people live, dress, and celebrate. Missionaries use the people's own way of life to share God's love with them.

SHARING FAITH
with My Family

Sharing What I Learned

Look at the pictures below. Use each picture to tell your family what you learned in this chapter.

For All to See

"Rejoice in the Lord always."
(Philippians 4:4)

Sharing and Showing Our Faith

Gather your family together. Have the family choose a holy day of the Church. Together fill out this chart.

Holy Day	How We Celebrate
_____	_____
_____	_____
_____	_____

Pray the Our Father together. As you pray, picture the people of the Church throughout the whole world. Some are praying the Our Father right now just as you are.

Visit Sadlier's

www.WeBelieveweb.com

Connect to the Catechism
For adult background and reflection, see paragraphs 831, 882, 886, and 2179.

24

We Pray

✝ We Gather in Prayer

Leader: The Lord be with you.

All: And also with you.

Leader: Lift up your hearts.

All: We lift them up to the Lord.

Leader: Let us give thanks to the Lord our God.

All: It is right to give him thanks and praise.

🎵 Sing Hosanna

Sing hosanna! Sing hosanna!
Sing it for Jesus. Sing it for Jesus.
Sing it for friendship.
Sing it for friendship.

Sing it forever. Sing it forever.
Sing hosanna! Sing hosanna!
Sing hosanna! Sing!

Play the conga! Play the conga!
Play it for Jesus. Play it for Jesus.
Play it for friendship.
Play it for friendship.

Play it forever. Play it forever.
Play the conga! Play the conga!
Play the conga drum!

Prayer keeps us close to God.

WE GATHER

✝ *God, help us to talk to you.*

Why do you talk to other people?
Why do you listen to other people?

WE BELIEVE

God wants us to get to know him better.
We can grow closer to God through prayer.
Prayer is talking and listening to God.
No matter how we pray, God is with us.

We talk to God about
different things. We talk
to him when we are
happy and when we are
sad. We share the things

prayer talking and listening to God

we are thinking about. Sometimes we ask
for help or forgiveness. Other times we
thank him for his love, or ask his blessing.

God is always there to hear our prayer.
He listens to us. He knows what we need
and takes care of us.

Prayer is more than talking to God. We
listen to God, too. God speaks to us in
many ways. He speaks to us at Mass
and through the sacraments. He
speaks to us through the words
of the Bible. He speaks to us
through the leaders of
Church and through all of
those who show us his love.

WE RESPOND

Follow this prayer path. Answer the questions and pray along the way.

PRAYER PATH

PARISH

Who helps you to grow as a disciple of Jesus?

_____

Ask God to bless all those who share their faith with you.

NEIGHBORHOOD

Who in your neighborhood is in need?

_____

Pray for those in need that they may have strength and the things they need.

GOD'S CREATION

What are some gifts of creation that you use and enjoy?

_____

Praise God for his gifts of creation.

273

Jesus prayed to God his Father.

WE GATHER

✝ *God, thank you for always listening to our prayers.*

 Circle the things that you do with your family. Add other things that you do.

Share a meal.

Learn about God.

Read a book.

Visit your relatives.

Go to the park.

Pray together.

_____   _____

Talk about why these things are important to families.

WE BELIEVE

Jesus, Mary, and Joseph were part of a family. When Jesus was growing up in Nazareth, he learned to pray. He prayed with Mary and Joseph. They prayed the prayers Jewish people had always prayed. They also gathered with other Jewish families to pray.

They all traveled to Jerusalem to celebrate religious holidays. The **Temple** is the holy place in Jerusalem where the Jewish people worshiped God.

As Jesus grew older he continued to pray. He wanted to be close to God his Father. He asked his Father to be with him. He thanked his Father for his many blessings.

Jesus often went off by himself to pray. Jesus also prayed when he was with his family, friends, and disciples.

Temple the holy place in Jerusalem where the Jewish people worshiped God

WE RESPOND

What are some times when you pray by yourself? How do you pray?

What are some times when you pray with others? How do you pray?

The Solitude of Christ, Maurice Denis, 1918

Jesus teaches us to pray.

WE GATHER

✝ *Jesus, help us to pray.*

Who are the people who have taught you to pray? What prayers did they teach you?

WE BELIEVE

Jesus' disciples knew that he loved and called on his Father. They saw how important prayer was to Jesus.

They wanted to learn how to pray as Jesus did. One day they asked Jesus, "Lord, teach us to pray." (Luke 11:1)

Jesus taught them this prayer.

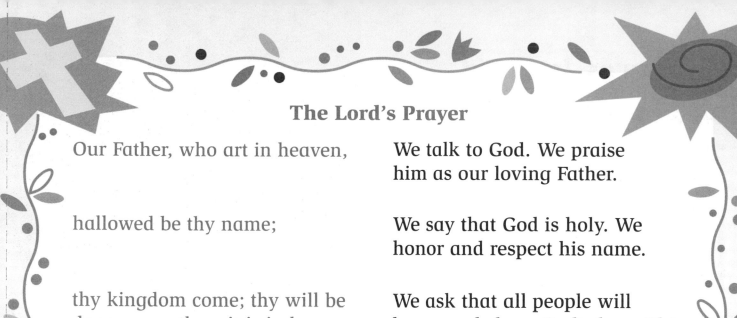

The Lord's Prayer

Our Father, who art in heaven,

We talk to God. We praise him as our loving Father.

hallowed be thy name;

We say that God is holy. We honor and respect his name.

thy kingdom come; thy will be done on earth as it is in heaven.

We ask that all people will know and share God's love. This is what God wants for all of us.

Give us this day our daily bread;

We ask God to give us what we need. We remember all people who are hungry or poor.

and forgive us our trespasses as we forgive those who
   trespass against us;

We ask God to forgive us. We need to forgive others.

and lead us not into temptation, but deliver us from evil. Amen.

We ask God to keep us safe from anything that goes against his love.

This prayer is called the Lord's Prayer. It is also called the Our Father.

WE RESPOND

Our actions can also be prayers. How can you use actions to pray?

As a class make up prayerful actions for each of the parts of the Our Father. Then pray the prayer using the actions.

We pray as Jesus did.

WE GATHER

✝ *Jesus, be with us when we pray.*

 Draw a picture of yourself praying.

WE BELIEVE

We pray by ourselves and with others as Jesus did. There are many reasons to pray. We pray:

- to ask God for help
- to tell God how beautiful the world is
- to ask God to forgive us for hurting others
- to pray for someone who needs help or is sick
- to thank God for his love
- to ask for God's blessing for us and others.

When we pray we can use our own words. We can also use prayers that we have learned at home, in school, or in our parish. We use many of these prayers when we pray together.

Praying together is an important part of being a member of the Church. As a parish we join together to celebrate the Eucharist and the other sacraments.

There are other times when our parish prays together. Talk about some of these times.

WE RESPOND

Think about one way you and your family will pray with your parish this week.

Now sit quietly. Talk and listen to God.

As Catholics...

At special times of the day, many members of the Church come together to pray. Morning and evening are two of these special times. At morning prayer and evening prayer, people gather to pray and sing psalms. They listen to readings from the Bible. They pray for the whole world. They thank God for his creation. Many religious communities gather in their chapels for morning and evening prayer. Your parish may gather, too.

Find out if your parish gathers to celebrate morning and evening prayer.

Circle the correct answer. Circle ? if you do not know the answer.

1. God speaks to us in many ways.

   Yes   No   ?

2. Jesus only prayed by himself.

   Yes   No   ?

3. Prayer is talking to God and listening to him, too.

   Yes   No   ?

4. The Hail Mary is the prayer Jesus taught his disciples.

   Yes   No   ?

5. Prayer is important because

   _____

   _____

ASSESSMENT Make a prayer calendar for this week. Write ways you will pray each day. At the end of the week, see how many different ways you talked to and listened to God.

We Respond in Faith

Reflect & Pray

I will pray the Our Father often because

_____

_____

_____

Key Words

prayer (p. 272)
Temple (p. 275)

Remember

- Prayer keeps us close to God.
- Jesus prayed to God his Father.
- Jesus teaches us to pray.
- We pray as Jesus did.

OUR CATHOLIC LIFE

Contemplative Life

Some men and women join religious communities to spend their days in prayer. They live and work in places called monasteries, abbeys, and convents. The work that they do provides for their food and the things they need to live.

They live a life of prayer. Together as a community they pray at different hours of the day. They sing psalms from the Bible. They give thanks and praise to God. They pray for the whole world. They also spend time alone thinking about and praying to God. The prayers of these religious communities are very important to the Church and the world.

SHARING FAITH
with My Family

Sharing What I Learned

Look at the pictures below. Use each picture to tell your family what you learned in this chapter.

For All to See

"Lord, teach us to pray."
(Luke 11:1)

With Thankful Hearts

At the end of each day this week, have each person in your family share the good things that happened that day. Record the responses in a family journal.

Evening Prayer

Every evening this week, pray the following prayer of thanks together. You can also say your own prayer.

Dear God, before we go to sleep,
we want to thank you
for this day so full of
your kindness and your joy.
We close our eyes to rest
safe in your loving care.

Visit Sadlier's

www.WeBelieveweb.com

 Connect to the Catechism
For adult background and reflection, see paragraphs 2560, 2599, 2759, and 2767.

25

We Honor Mary and the Saints

✝ We Gather in Prayer

🎵 **Litany of Saints**

Holy Mary, Mother of God,
Holy Mary, born without sin,
Holy Mary, taken into heaven:

Chorus
Pray for us.
Pray with us.
Help us to share God's love.

Saint Peter and Saint Paul,
Saint Mary Magdalene,
Saint Catherine of Siena: (Chorus)

The Church honors the saints.

WE GATHER

✝ *Jesus, thank you for the people who show us your love.*

What does it mean to honor someone? What are some ways we honor people?

_____

_____

_____

Saint Catherine of Siena

Saint John Bosco

WE BELIEVE

God is good and holy and wants us to be holy, too. So he shares his life with us especially in the sacraments. The sacraments help us to be holy. Loving God and others helps us to be holy, too.

The Church community honors holy people. The saints are holy people. The **saints** are all the members of the Church who have died and are happy with God forever in heaven.

The saints loved God very much. They followed Jesus' example. They were kind and caring. They shared God's love with others.

284

We remember what the saints did and try to follow their example. Here are some of the saints we remember.

- Saint Peter and Saint Paul helped the Church to spread and grow.

- Saint Brigid of Ireland and Saint Catherine of Siena were peacemakers.

- Saint Rose of Lima and Saint Martin de Porres helped the poor and the sick.

- Saint John Bosco and Saint Frances Cabrini began schools to teach children about God's love.

How can you follow their example?

saints all the members of the Church who have died and are happy with God forever in heaven

Saint Frances Cabrini

WE RESPOND

Who are some of the other saints you have learned about?

Write one of the saints' names on the line.

_____

Write a sentence to tell how you will follow this person's example.

_____

_____

The Church honors Mary.

WE GATHER

✝ *God, help us to be holy.*

Share some things you have learned about Mary, the mother of Jesus.

WE BELIEVE

God chose Mary to be the mother of his own Son, Jesus. So God blessed her in a special way. Mary was free from sin from the very first moment of her life. She was always filled with grace. All through her life she did what God wanted.

A few months before Jesus was born, God sent an angel to Mary.

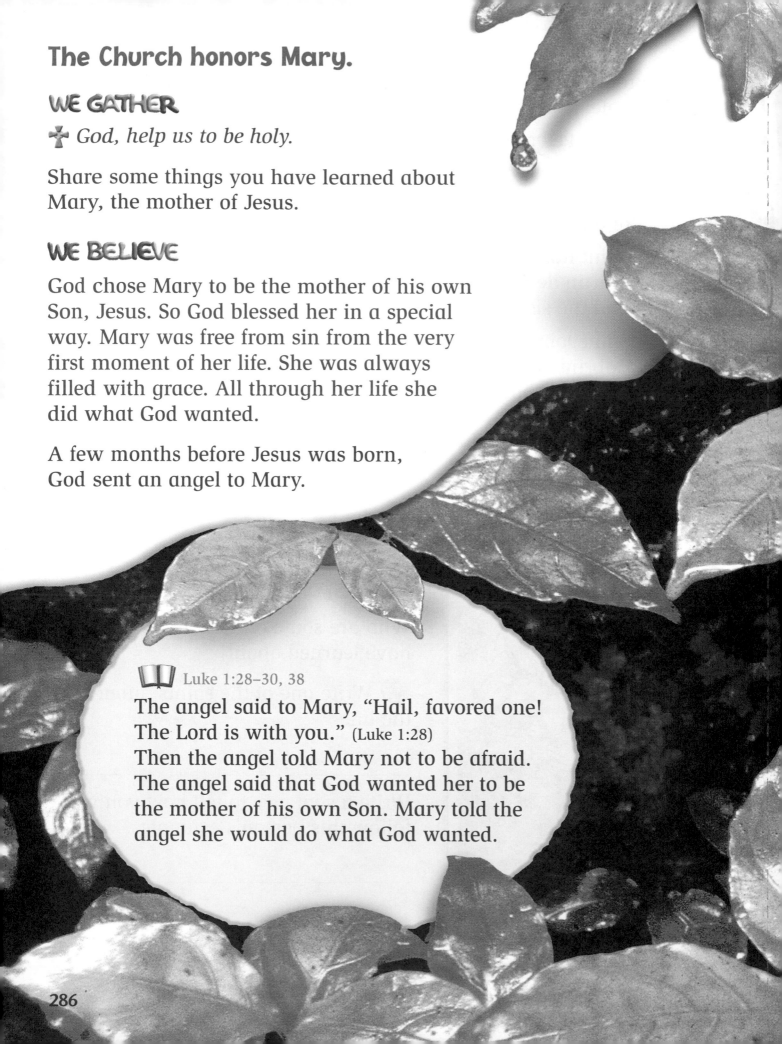

📖 Luke 1:28–30, 38

The angel said to Mary, "Hail, favored one! The Lord is with you." (Luke 1:28)
Then the angel told Mary not to be afraid. The angel said that God wanted her to be the mother of his own Son. Mary told the angel she would do what God wanted.

286

Mary is Jesus' mother. Jesus loved and honored her. We love and honor Mary as our mother, too. Mary is a holy woman. She is the greatest of saints. She is an example for all of Jesus' disciples.

Virgin and Child Enthroned, Sister Corita Kent c. 1960

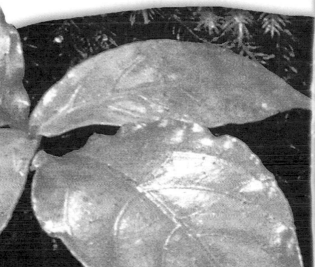
Use this code to find what we sometimes call Mary.

B	D	E	H	L	M	O	R	S	T
1	2	3	4	5	6	7	8	9	10

We call Mary the

___ ___ ___ ___ ___ ___ ___
1   5   3   9   9   3   2

___ ___ ___ ___ ___ ___.
6   7   10   4   3   8

WE RESPOND

How can we honor Mary as the greatest saint?

Pray quietly. Thank Mary for being the mother of the Son of God.

We honor Mary with special prayers.

WE GATHER

✠ *Holy Mary, we love you.*

What do families do to get ready for babies before they are born?

WE BELIEVE

Mary had a cousin named Elizabeth. Elizabeth was older than Mary. Elizabeth was going to have a baby, too. Mary went to visit her cousin and help her.

📖 Luke 1:39, 40–42

When Elizabeth saw Mary, she was very happy and excited. The Holy Spirit helped Elizabeth to know that God had chosen Mary to be the mother of his own Son.

Elizabeth said to Mary, "Most blessed are you among women, and blessed is the fruit of your womb." (Luke 1:42) These words to Mary are part of one of the Church's prayers. We call this prayer the Hail Mary.

Add your own decorations to the prayer frame. Underline Elizabeth's words to Mary.

Hail Mary

Hail Mary, full of grace,
the Lord is with you!
Blessed are you among women,
and blessed is the fruit of your womb,
 Jesus.
Holy Mary, Mother of God,
pray for us sinners,
now and at the hour of our death.
Amen.

As Catholics...

The rosary is a prayer in honor of Mary. When we pray the rosary, we use beads as we pray. We begin with the Sign of the Cross, the Apostles' Creed, Our Father, three Hail Marys, and a Glory to the Father. Then there are five sets of ten beads to pray Hail Marys. Each set begins with the Our Father and ends with the Glory to the Father.

As we pray each set of ten beads, we think about the lives of Jesus and Mary.

Plan a time this week to pray the rosary with your family.

WE RESPOND

What do you think Elizabeth's words to Mary might be today?

Pray the Hail Mary now.

We honor Mary on special days.

WE GATHER

✝ *Blessed Mother of God, pray for us.*

What are some different ways families thank mothers and grandmothers for all that they do?

WE BELIEVE

Catholics honor Mary in different ways during the year. On special days, called feast days, the whole parish gathers for Mass. Here are some of Mary's feast days.

Date	We gather to celebrate
January 1	Mary is the Mother of God.
August 15	Mary is in heaven with God forever.
December 8	Mary was free from sin from the very first moment of her life.

Sometimes parish communities gather to honor Mary in special ways. They may have a procession. A **procession** is a prayer walk. While walking, people pray and sing. On December 12, many parishes have a procession to honor Mary as Our Lady of Guadalupe.

Key Word

procession a prayer walk

Inside and outside homes and churches, people often put statues and pictures of Mary. Looking at the statues and pictures can help people to remember Mary.

WE RESPOND

🎵 Immaculate Mary

Immaculate Mary,
your praises we sing.
You reign now in heaven
with Jesus our King.
Ave, Ave, Ave, Maria!
Ave, Ave, Maria!

🧍 What can your class do to honor Mary? Write your ideas.

_____

_____

_____

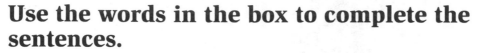

Use the words in the box to complete the sentences.

Elizabeth	Saints	Hail Mary	honor	Mary

1. _____ is the greatest saint.

2. The _____ is one of the Church's prayers to honor Mary.

3. Feast days and processions are ways to

   _____ Mary.

4. _____ are all the members of the Church who have died and are happy with God forever in heaven.

Answer this question.

5. Why do we remember the saints?

_____

Make a chart. List the ways parishes honor Mary and the saints. Draw pictures and write sentences.

We Respond in Faith

Reflect & Pray

Saints show us ways to be holy. They

_____

_____

_____ .

God, thank you for the example of

_____ .

Key Words

saints (p. 285)
procession (p. 290)

Remember

- The Church honors the saints.
- The Church honors Mary.
- We honor Mary with special prayers.
- We honor Mary on special days.

OUR CATHOLIC LIFE

Works of Art

Our churches have always been filled with beautiful works of art. Paintings and stained-glass windows have shown scenes from the life of Jesus or from the lives of the saints. By telling stories through pictures, artists teach us about what Jesus, the Blessed Mother, and the saints did. Looking at these works of art helps us to pray.

SHARING FAITH with My Family

Sharing What I Learned

Look at the pictures below. Use each picture to tell your family what you learned in this chapter.

For All to See

"Most blessed are you among women."
(Luke 1:42)

Saints' Hall of Fame

Plan together a "Saints' Hall of Fame." Ask each family member to name a favorite saint. Have each person tell why they chose that saint. Talk about the ways you can follow the example of the saints.

A Litany of Saints

Add your favorite saints.

Holy Mary, pray for us.
Saint Joseph, pray for us.
Saint Peter, pray for us.
Saint Elizabeth Ann Seton, pray for us.

Saint _____, pray for us.
All holy men and women, pray for us.

Visit Sadlier's
www.WEBELIEVEweb.com

Connect to the Catechism
For adult background and reflection, see paragraphs 957, 963, 971, and 2676.

We Show Love and Respect

✝ We Gather in Prayer

Leader: Let us listen to these words from one of Saint Paul's letters.

Reader: "Love is patient, love is kind. Love never fails. Faith, hope, love remain, these three; but the greatest of these is love."

(1 Corinthians 13:4, 8, 13)

The word of the Lord.

All: Thanks be to God.

Leader: Now let us form a circle and sing.

🎵 A Circle of Love

Chorus

A circle of love, yes a circle of love;
each hand in a hand, a circle of
    friends.
A circle of love that is open to all;
we open the circle and welcome
    each one of you in.

Each person has something to bring:
a song, a story, a smile, a teardrop,
a dream, and loving to share. (Chorus)

We live in God's love.

WE GATHER

✝ *God, fill us with your love.*

When do people give gifts?
Why do they give gifts?

WE BELIEVE

The world we live in is God's gift to us. God has given us many gifts. He has given us creation. He has given us laws to know and love him. He has given us his word in the Bible. He has given us the Church to help and guide us.

However, God's greatest gift is the gift of his Son, Jesus. Jesus gives us a share in God's life and love. We call this grace. We receive grace each time we celebrate the sacraments. We are strengthened by the Holy Spirit. We are filled with the gifts of faith, hope, and love.

The gift of faith helps us to believe in God—the Father, the Son, and the Holy Spirit. We believe in God and all that he has done for us.

The gift of hope makes it easier to trust. We trust in Jesus and in God's promise to love us always.

296

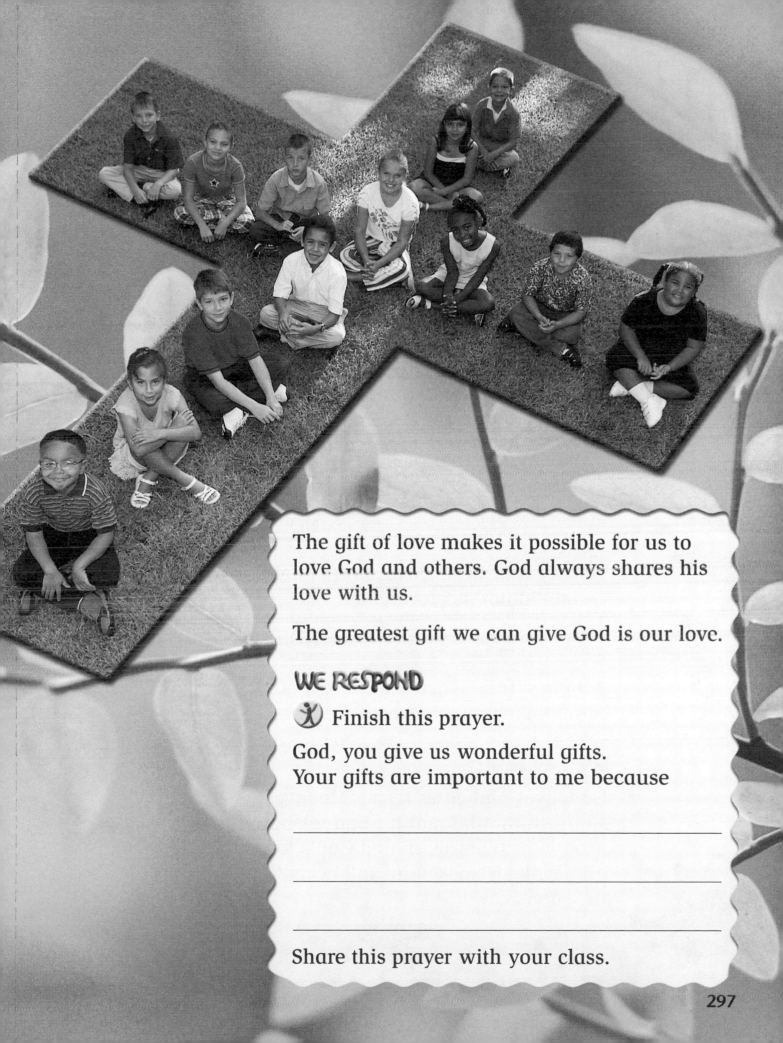

The gift of love makes it possible for us to love God and others. God always shares his love with us.

The greatest gift we can give God is our love.

WE RESPOND

Finish this prayer.

God, you give us wonderful gifts.
Your gifts are important to me because

_____

_____

_____

Share this prayer with your class.

Jesus taught us to love others.

WE GATHER

✝ *Jesus, we praise you for your love.*

🏃 Do you think these things would set a good example for others? Circle YES or NO.

- Joshua and his four-year-old brother share a room. When Joshua comes home, he always throws his clothes and books all over the room.

  YES   NO

- Vanessa sees her older sister pray before Mass starts.

  YES   NO

- Ricky raked the leaves for his neighbor and did not ask for money.

  YES   NO

Act out a time when you were a good example for someone else.

WE BELIEVE

God loves and cares for us. He loves us so much that he sent his Son to share his love with us. Jesus shared God's love with all people. He asked his followers to do the same.

Jesus taught his followers to love God and one another. He showed us the way to:

- pray to the Father
- live as a family
- be a friend and neighbor
- love and respect those who were poor, sick, and lonely.

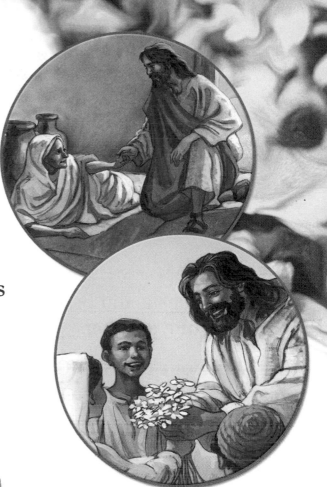

Look at these pictures of Jesus. How is Jesus showing love? How can you follow Jesus' example?

Jesus spent a lot of time talking with his followers. He loved them very much. He asked them to follow his example of love.

 John 13:34–35

Jesus said, "I give you a new commandment: love one another. As I have loved you, so you also should love one another. This is how all will know that you are my disciples, if you have love for one another." (John 13:34–35)

Jesus' **new commandment** is to love one another as he has loved us.

WE RESPOND

What will you do this week to show you are a disciple of Jesus?

Key Word

new commandment Jesus' commandment to love one another as he has loved us

299

We love and respect others.

WE GATHER

✝ *Holy Spirit, help us to live as Jesus did.*

Who are some of the people you love?
What are some signs of your love for them?

WE BELIEVE

Loving as Jesus did brings us closer to
God and one another.

We show our belief in God by loving and
respecting him. We honor God's name as
a sign of our love. Together we worship
God. We remember all his gifts. We thank
God for all he has done for us.

Following Jesus' new commandment helps
us to follow all of God's commandments.

Circle every third letter to finish Jesus' new commandment. Write the words on the lines.

B I L T C O P L V S X E Q Z D   A G Y N F O S I U

A B L E I O P S V Z Y E   U T O W A N L I E

Y E A R S N Q U O H E T R C H I O E L M R

"As I have __ __ __ __ __   __ __ __,

so you also should __ __ __ __   __ __ __

__ __ __ __ __ __ __." (John 13:34)

When we follow Jesus' words, we try to love our family, friends, and all people as he did. We respect and obey our parents and all those who take care of us. We thank our families and friends for their love and help. We also try to be kind, fair, and truthful. We share the things we have. We respect the belongings of other people.

WE RESPOND

Sit quietly and think about ways you can follow Jesus' new commandment.

I will follow Jesus' new commandment today by

_____

We respect God's creation.

WE GATHER

✝ *God, what wonders are in your creation!*

What are some things that you take care of? What are some things your family takes care of? What things do people in your neighborhood take care of?

WE BELIEVE

God asks us to respect his gift of creation. God created the land and the sea, the sun, moon, and stars. God created all the animals and plants. He created us, too! All that God created is good.

🎵 God Made the World

God made the world so broad and grand,
  filled it with blessings from his hand.
God made the sky so high and blue,
  and all the little children too.

God made the sun, the moon and stars,
  lighting the world from near and far.
God made the world with tender care
  and all the little children there.

God made the sparrow and the rose,
  gifts for the ear, the eye and nose.
God made the beauty voices bring,
  when all the little
  children sing.

People have a special place in God's creation. God has asked us to take care of his gifts of creation.

We care for the world. We protect all that God created. We work together to share the goodness of creation.

We can find the things God created in our backyards, our neighborhoods, our cities, and in every country. The gifts of God's creation are everywhere!

WE RESPOND

Put a check (✓) in front of the ways you will take care of God's creation this week.

☐ feed and care for my pet

☐ put trash in a can

☐ recycle cans, bottles, and papers

☐ turn off the water

☐ plant new trees

Now add two more ways you will help care for creation next week.

_____

_____

Fill in the circle beside the correct answer.

1. Jesus shared God's love with _____ people.

   ○ all   ○ a few   ○ some

2. Jesus' new commandment is to love one another as _____ loved us.

   ○ his followers   ○ his neighbors   ○ he

3. _____ have a special place in God's creation.

   ○ Plants   ○ People   ○ Animals

4. God's greatest gift to us is his _____.

   ○ Son   ○ creation   ○ law

Write your answer.

5. The gifts of faith, hope, and love help us

   _____

   _____

Use pictures or words to show ways people can follow Jesus' new commandment.

We Respond in Faith

Reflect & Pray

Jesus, you show us

_____

_____

_____

Thank you for sharing your life and love with us.

Key Word

new commandment (p. 299)

Remember

- We live in God's love.
- Jesus taught us to love others.
- We love and respect others.
- We respect God's creation.

OUR CATHOLIC LIFE

Tell your story here.

Place your photo here.

SHARING FAITH
with My Family

Sharing What I Learned

Look at the pictures below. Use each picture to tell your family what you learned in this chapter.

For All to See and Pray

Paste a photo of your family or draw their picture in the empty space. Gather your family together. Read these words from one of Saint Paul's letters.

> "Love is patient,
> love is kind.
> It is not jealous . . .
> it is not rude . . .
> it does not rejoice over
> wrongdoing but rejoices
> with the truth."
>
> (1 Corinthians 13:4, 5, 6)

Talk about what the words mean for your family.

My Family

Visit Sadlier's
www.WeBelieveweb.com

Connect to the Catechism
For adult background and reflection, see paragraphs 307, 1694, 1823, and 1825.

Easter

Christ has risen, Alleluia!

Easter is a season to celebrate the Resurrection of Jesus.

WE GATHER

How do you show you are happy?
Act out some things you do.

WE BELIEVE

The Three Days lead us to the Easter season. The Easter season is a time of rejoicing. This season lasts fifty days.

During the Easter season, we celebrate that Jesus rose from the dead. We give thanks for the new life he brings us.

Take part in the Easter celebration.

Leader: All during the season of Easter, the Church sings the song of "Alleluia." Alleluia means "Praise God!" Let us praise God now.

Leader (singing): Alleluia, alleluia, alleluia!

All (repeat): Alleluia, alleluia, alleluia!

📖 Luke 24:1-9

Reader 1: On the first day of the week, at dawn, the women went to the tomb. They were bringing spices to bless Jesus' body. They found the stone rolled away. The body of Jesus was gone!

Reader 2: While they stood there, two angels appeared beside them. The women were frightened.

Angel 1: Are you looking for Jesus? He is not here. He has been raised up.

Angel 2: Remember what Jesus told you. He said that he would give his life for us. He would be crucified. He said that on the third day he would rise again.

Reader 3: Then the women were filled with joy. They ran back to tell the other disciples what they had seen and heard.

All (singing): Alleluia, alleluia, alleluia!

Like the women at the tomb, we go and tell others about Jesus' Resurrection. We want them to know the good news that Jesus died and rose for all people. We want to share the joy that comes from believing in Jesus.

WE RESPOND

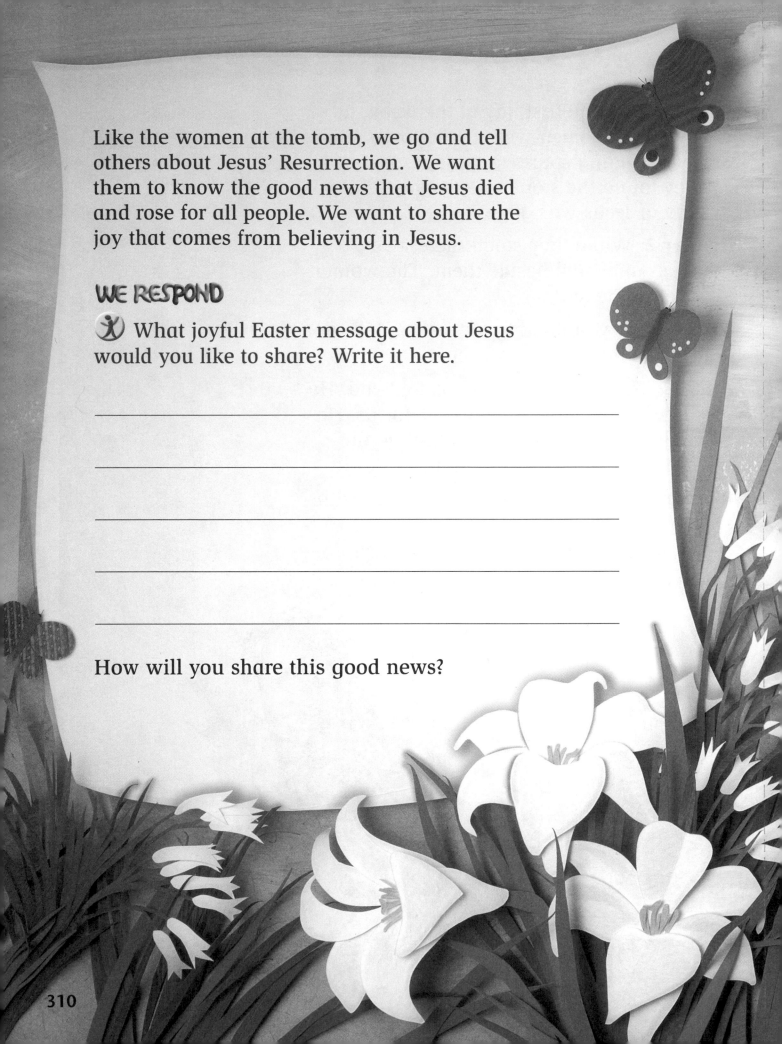 What joyful Easter message about Jesus would you like to share? Write it here.

_____

_____

_____

_____

_____

How will you share this good news?

✝ We Respond in Prayer

Leader: Jesus, we know you are alive and with us today. Alleluia!

Reader 1: Give thanks to the Lord, for he is good, for his mercy lasts forever, alleluia!

All: This is the day the Lord has made; let us rejoice and be glad.

Reader 2: Set your heart on Jesus Christ, for he is risen, alleluia!

All: This is the day the Lord has made; let us rejoice and be glad.

Reader 3: This we believe, alleluia, alleluia, alleluia!

All: This is the day the Lord has made; let us rejoice and be glad.

🎵 **This Is the Day**

This is the day, this is the day
that the Lord has made,
that the Lord has made;
we will rejoice, we will rejoice and
be glad in it, and be glad in it.

This is the day
that the Lord has made;
we will rejoice
and be glad in it.
This is the day, this is the
day that the Lord has made.

SHARING FAITH
with My Family

Sharing What I Learned

Look at the pictures below. Use each picture to tell your family what you learned in this chapter.

Family Prayer

During the Easter season, the Church often prays three alleluias in a row, instead of just one. Add Easter joy to meal prayers or evening prayers. Try praying three alleluias after the Amen. Alleluia, alleluia, alleluia!

For All to See and Pray

Share the joy that comes from believing in Jesus. Draw signs of new life on the Alleluia banner. Put the banner in a place where you will see it often.

Alleluia!

Visit Sadlier's
www.WeBelieveweb.com

Connect to the Catechism
For adult background and reflection, see paragraph 641.

SHARING FAITH

in Class and at Home

Look at the Picture

- Circle all the clues, or signs, in the picture that help tell you what the family is doing.

- Why do you think families celebrate?

_____

_____

Because *We Believe*

Spending time together is one way that families show their love. Being together helps family members to grow closer and know they belong to one another.

In our parish family we spend time together every week for Mass and at special times throughout the year. We celebrate our love for God and for one another. We share God's life and love with our families and with other people.

We celebrate the sacraments with our parish family. We grow stronger in our faith. We grow as followers of Jesus.

How do we show we believe this?

"Love one another as I love you."

John 15:12

313

Catholics celebrate God's love by praying and worshiping together.

With Your Class

Each week our parish family gathers to celebrate at Mass. Finish this sentence together with a partner to describe what we do at Mass.

At Mass we _____

With Your Family

Read page 313 together. Talk about the ways families celebrate together. How does our parish family celebrate together at Mass?

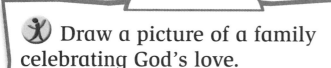 Draw a picture of a family celebrating God's love.

"It is the whole community, the Body of Christ . . . that celebrates."

(Catechism of the Catholic Church, 1140)

Pray Together

**Dear God,
We are thankful for our family. When we are together, help us to**

_____

Amen.

SHARING FAITH
in Class and at Home

When It is Hard to Forgive

Diana and Desiree are twin sisters. Desiree has taken out Diana's favorite puzzle and has not put it back. When Diana sees the pieces all over the bedroom floor, she is angry. "Desiree," she yells, "you are lazy, and you never take care of anything."

Desiree starts to cry. "Diana, you are always mean to me. You never share."

What Do You Think?

• Why are Diana and Desiree upset?

• Why is it important to forgive?

 Talk about what will happen next.

Because *We Believe*

Families do not always get along. When we forgive, we can come back together again. This is called reconciliation.

Jesus told stories to help us understand how important it is to be forgiving. Jesus wants us to forgive each other. Jesus loved and respected all people. He wants us to treat others with love and respect.

How do we show that we believe this?

> "As the Lord has forgiven you, so must you also do."
> Colossians 3:13

God's love and forgiveness gives us peace. When we forgive others, we give them peace, too.

With Your Class

Choose an area in your classroom that can be used as a "peace place" to sit and talk. Use your "peace place" to settle differences, or just to feel some peace.

What are some ways that you can be peacemakers in your school?

With Your Family

Read page 315 together. Talk about ways we can learn to forgive in our family.

"Each and everyone should be generous and tireless in forgiving one another."

(Catechism of the Catholic Church, 2227)

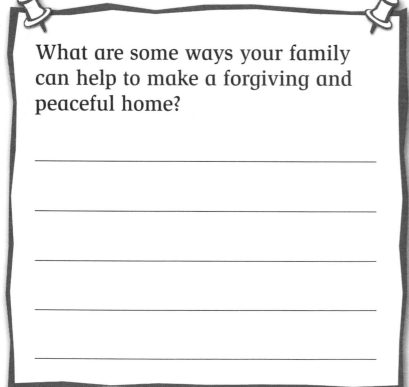

What are some ways your family can help to make a forgiving and peaceful home?

_____

_____

_____

_____

_____

Pray Together

**Lord Jesus,
May your peace take root in our heart and bring forth a harvest of love, holiness, and truth.
Amen.**

NOW WHAT?
Bring this page back to school ☐   Keep this page at home ☐

Remembering Someone Special

Pedro wanted to remember all that happened at the celebration for his grandmother. So he drew pictures of the celebration.

- Why does Pedro draw the pictures?
- How do you remember someone special?

Because *We Believe*

Before he died, Jesus shared a special meal with his disciples. We call this meal the Last Supper. At this meal, bread and wine became the Body and Blood of Jesus.

We celebrate the Last Supper at the Eucharist. We listen to God's word and receive the Body and Blood of Jesus. We remember how much Jesus loves us and wants us to love one another.

When we share the Eucharist, we remember that we are joined to Christ and to one another.

How do we show that we believe this?

"This is my body which will be given for you; do this in memory of me."

Luke 22:19

Here are Pedro's drawings.

Here is Nana!

She opens a gift from Uncle Marcos

Wow! It's a camera!

We love each other so much!

317

The Mass is the celebration
of the Eucharist.

At Mass we also remember others.
We pray for people in our
community and around the world.

With Your Class

Work in small groups to write a
prayer for people in our community
or around the world.

With Your Family

Read page 317 together. Talk about
the ways the Eucharist helps us
remember that Jesus loves us and
wants us to care for one another.

Think of something that reminds you
of a special time or person in your family.

**"The family is the 'domestic
church' where God's children
learn to pray 'as the Church'
and to persevere in prayer."**

(Catechism of the Catholic Church, 2685)

Write about your memories here.

Pray Together

**Pray the Our
Father together.**

NOW WHAT?
Bring this page back to school ☐   Keep this page at home ☐

Fill in the circle beside each correct answer.

1. A _____ is an area of the Church led by a bishop.

   ○ diocese   ○ parish   ○ neighborhood

2. _____ is talking and listening to God.

   ○ Penance   ○ Prayer   ○ Temple

3. The greatest saint is _____.

   ○ Mary   ○ Elizabeth   ○ Joseph

4. The pope is the leader of the whole Church.

   ○ Yes   ○ No

5. The Our Father is a prayer to honor Mary.

   ○ Yes   ○ No

6. The saints are happy with God in heaven.

   ○ Yes   ○ No

7–8. Write two ways the Church honors Mary.

_____

9–10. Write two ways that we show we respect God's creation.

_____

Complete the crossword puzzle.

Across

1. talking and listening to God

2. members of the Church who have died and are happy with God forever in heaven

Down

1. the priest who leads and serves the parish

3. a holy place where Jewish people worship God

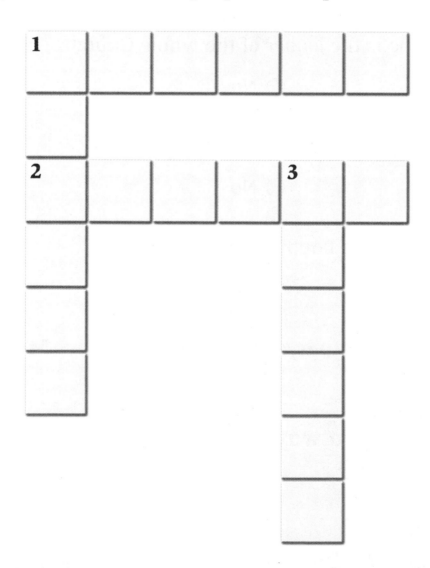

My Mass Book

The priest blesses us.
The priest or deacon says,
"Go in peace to love and
serve the Lord."
We say,
"Thanks be to God."
We go out to live as
Jesus' followers.

We welcome one another.
We stand and sing.
We pray the Sign of the Cross.
The priest says,
"The Lord be with you."
We answer,
"And also with you."

We gather with our parish. We remember and celebrate what Jesus said and did at the Last Supper.

Cut on this line.

2

Fold on this line.

15

We ask God and one another for forgiveness.
We praise God as we sing,

"Glory to God in the highest, and peace to his people on earth."

4

Then the priest invites us to share in the Eucharist. As people receive the Body and Blood of Christ, they answer,

"Amen."

While this is happening, we sing a song of thanks.

13

We get ready to receive Jesus.
Together we pray or sing the
Our Father. Then we share a
sign of peace.
We say,
"Peace be with you."

The Liturgy of the Word

We listen to two readings from
the Bible.
After each one, the reader says,
"The word of the Lord."
We answer,
"Thanks be to God."

Then the priest takes the
cup of wine.
He says,
"Take this, all of you, and
drink from it: this is the cup
of my blood. . . ."

We stand to say aloud what
we believe as Catholics.
Then we pray for the Church
and all people.
After each prayer we say,
"Lord, hear our prayer."

We stand and sing **Alleluia.**
The priest or deacon reads the gospel.
Then he says,
"The Gospel of the Lord."
We answer,
**"Praise to you,
Lord Jesus Christ."**

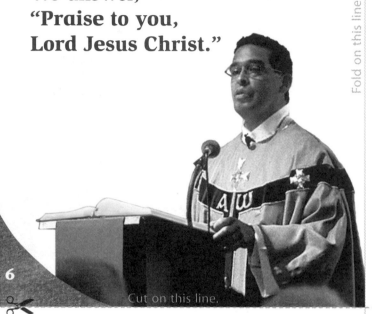

Cut on this line.

Fold on this line.

We sing or pray,

"Amen."

We believe Jesus Christ is really present in the Eucharist.

The Liturgy of the Eucharist

With the priest, we prepare the altar.
People bring gifts of bread and wine to the altar.
The priest prepares these gifts.
We pray,
"Blessed be God for ever."

Then we remember what Jesus said and did at the Last Supper.
The priest takes the bread.
He says,
"Take this, all of you, and eat it: this is my body which will be given up for you."

My Prayer Book

Fold on this line.

Cut on this line.

The Apostles' Creed

I believe in God the
    Father almighty,
    creator of heaven and earth.

I believe in Jesus Christ,
    his only Son, our Lord.
    He was conceived by the power
    of the Holy Spirit
    and born of the Virgin Mary.
    He suffered under Pontius Pilate,
    was crucified, died and
    was buried.
    He descended to the dead.
    On the third day he rose again.

Glory to the Father

Glory to the Father,
    and to the Son,
    and to the Holy Spirit:
as it was in the beginning,
    is now, and will be forever.

Amen.

Sign of the Cross

In the name of the Father,
and of the Son,
and of the Holy Spirit.

Amen.

Fold on this line.

Cut on this line.

He ascended into heaven,
and is seated at the right hand
of the Father.
He will come again to judge
the living and the dead.

I believe in the Holy Spirit,
the holy catholic Church,
the communion of saints,
the forgiveness of sins,
the resurrection of the body,
and the life everlasting.

Amen.

Our Father

Our Father, who art in heaven,
hallowed be thy name;
thy kingdom come;
thy will be done on earth as
it is in heaven.
Give us this day our daily bread;
and forgive us our trespasses
as we forgive those who
trespass against us;
and lead us not into temptation,
but deliver us from evil.

Amen.

Grace After Meals

We give you thanks
almighty God
for these and all your gifts,
which we have received through
Christ our Lord.

Amen.

Grace Before Meals

Bless us, O Lord, and these
   your gifts
which we are about to receive
from your goodness.
Through Christ our Lord.

Amen.

Fold on this line.

Hail Mary

Hail Mary, full of grace,
the Lord is with you!
Blessed are you among women,
and blessed is the fruit of your
   womb, Jesus.
Holy Mary, mother of God,
pray for us sinners,
now and at the hour of
   our death.

Amen.

Morning Offering

My God, I offer you today
all that I think and do and say,
uniting it with what was done
on earth, by Jesus Christ,
your Son.

I firmly intend, with your help,
to do penance,
to sin no more,
and to avoid whatever
   leads me to sin.
Our Savior Jesus Christ
suffered and died for us.
In his name, my God,
   have mercy.

Act of Contrition

My God,
I am sorry for my sins with
    all my heart.
In choosing to do wrong
and failing to do good,
I have sinned against you
whom I should love above
    all things.

Fold on this line.

Cut on this line.

Evening Prayer

Dear God, before I sleep
I want to thank you for this day
so full of your kindness
and your joy.
I close my eyes to rest
safe in your loving care.

Prayer Before the Blessed Sacrament

Jesus,
You are God-with-us,
especially in this sacrament
of the Eucharist.
You love me as I am
and help me grow.

Come and be with me
in all my joys and sorrows.
Help me share your peace
and love
with everyone I meet.
I ask in your name.

Amen.

The Seven Sacraments

The Sacraments of Christian Initiation
Baptism

Confirmation

Eucharist

The Sacraments of Healing
Penance and Reconciliation

Anointing of the Sick

The Sacraments at the Service of Communion
Holy Orders

Matrimony

The Ten Commandments

1. I am the LORD your God: you shall not have strange gods before me.
2. You shall not take the name of the LORD your God in vain.
3. Remember to keep holy the LORD's Day.
4. Honor your father and your mother.
5. You shall not kill.
6. You shall not commit adultery.
7. You shall not steal.
8. You shall not bear false witness against your neighbor.
9. You shall not covet your neighbor's wife.
10. You shall not covet your neighbor's goods.

Glossary

absolution (page 145)
God's forgiveness of our sins by the priest in the sacrament of Reconciliation

anointing with oil (page 73)
tracing a cross on the person's forehead with oil during Confirmation

apostles (page 33)
the twelve men chosen by Jesus to be the leaders of his disciples

assembly (page 189)
the community of people who join together for the celebration of the Mass

Baptism (page 59)
the sacrament in which we are freed from sin and given grace

Bible (page 97)
the book in which God's word is written

bishops (page 263)
leaders of the Church who carry on the work of the apostles

Blessed Sacrament (page 222)
another name for the Eucharist

Blessed Trinity (page 26)
the three Persons in one God

called by God (page 249)
invited by God to love and serve him

Catholics (page 45)
baptized members of the Church, led and guided by the pope and bishops

Church (page 39)
all the people who are baptized in Jesus Christ and follow his teachings

commandments (page 109)
God's laws

confession (page 145)
telling our sins to the priest in the sacrament of Reconciliation

Confirmation (page 70)
the sacrament that seals us with the Gift of the Holy Spirit and strengthens us

conscience (page 136)
God's gift that helps us to know right from wrong

contrition (page 145)
being sorry for our sins and promising not to sin again

diocese (page 263)
an area of the Church led by a bishop

disciples (page 33)
those who follow Jesus

divine (page 25)
a word used to describe God

Eucharist (page 176)
the sacrament of the Body and Blood of Jesus Christ

eucharistic prayer (page 210)
the most important prayer of the Mass

faith (page 47)
a gift from God that helps us to trust God and believe in him

free will (page 122)
God's gift to us that allows us to make choices

gospels (page 101)
four of the books in the New Testament that are about Jesus' teachings and his life on earth

grace (page 59)
God's life in us

Great Commandment (page 109)
Jesus' teaching to love God and others

Holy Communion (page 179)
receiving the Body and Blood of Christ

Holy Family (page 20)
the family of Jesus, Mary, and Joseph

homily (page 201)
the talk given by the priest or deacon at Mass that helps us understand the readings and how we are to live

Last Supper (page 175)
the meal Jesus shared with his disciples on the night before he died

Liturgy of the Eucharist (page 209)
the second main part of the Mass in which the gifts of bread and wine become the Body and Blood of Christ

New Testament (page 101)
the second part of the Bible

Old Testament (page 99)
the first part of the Bible

original sin (page 59)
the first man and woman disobeyed God; the first sin

parishes (page 45)
communities that worship and work together

pastor (page 261)
the priest who leads and serves the parish

a penance (page 145)
a prayer or kind act we do to make up for our sins

Penance and Reconciliation (page 135)
the sacrament in which we receive and celebrate God's forgiveness of our sins

pope (page 264)
the leader of the Church who continues the work of Saint Peter

prayer (page 272)
talking and listening to God

procession (page 290)
a prayer walk

psalm (page 198)
a song of praise from the Bible

Liturgy of the Word (page 197)
the first main part of the Mass when we listen to God's word

Mass (page 179)
the celebration of the Eucharist

mercy (page 126)
God's love and forgiveness

mortal sins (page 124)
sins that break our friendship with God

new commandment (page 299)
Jesus' commandment to love one another as he has loved us

Resurrection (page 35)
Jesus' rising from the dead

sacrament (page 48)
a special sign given to us by Jesus

saints (page 285)
all the members of the Church who have died and are happy with God forever in heaven

sin (page 124)
a thought, word, or act that we freely choose to commit even though we know that it is wrong

tabernacle (page 222)
the special place in the church in which the Blessed Sacrament is kept

Temple (page 275)
the holy place in Jerusalem where the Jewish people worshiped God

Ten Commandments (page 110)
ten special laws God gave to his people

venial sins (page 124)
sins that hurt our friendship with God

worship (page 47)
to give God thanks and praise

Index

The following is a list of topics that appear in the pupil's text.
Boldface indicates an entire chapter.